Practical NLP 2: Languagе

How to Use Presuppositions, Chunking, the Meta Model and the Milton Model in Practice

ANDY SMITH

Copyright © 2022 ANDY SMITH

All rights reserved.

CONTENTS

1	Introduction	1
2	'Deep Structure' And 'Surface Structure'	7
3	Presuppositions	11
4	The Hierarchy of Ideas ('Chunking')	31
5	The Meta Model	45
6	The Milton Model	79
7	Metaphors	123
8	How To Learn More	133
	Index	137
	About The Author	141

1 INTRODUCTION

What this book is about

This book covers a basic building block of NLP - the 'linguistic' part of Neuro-Linguistic Programming. It's all about language, and how language structures and sequences internal representations in your mind, and the mind of your listener or reader.

If you would like a deeper understanding of the structure of language, and how the words we use and hear act as a filter on incoming information, and direct attention to particular aspects of our experience, read on.

By the end of this book you'll be more able to read between the lines of what people say, and to get some clues about what they believe and the rules they operate by, even when they don't explicitly state those rules. Would that be worth knowing about? Would it be useful to be able to detect the unspoken assumptions in people's language, for example if you are interviewing someone to join your team, or finding out about someone's requirements in a sales meeting or data gathering interview? Or even to get a better idea of what people are really looking for when you're sitting in a job interview, or wanting to demonstrate that you're ready to move up to the next level?

We will also be getting a deeper understanding of how our minds structure information, some side effects of using abstract, conceptual words that you may not have realised, some strategies for dealing with feeling overwhelmed and also for being more creative, and how to get past the number one limitation that stops people from rising above a certain level in their organisation, or from growing their business above a certain size.

So by the end of this book you will much more aware of the effect that your words are having, so you can use language much more precisely and appropriately to communicate with all kinds of people in a way that they can understand, and motivate them to do what you need them to do.

What is NLP?

You could think of Neuro-Linguistic Programming (NLP) as an owner's manual for the human brain. It's the study of how we think, feel and act, marked by an intense curiosity about how (rather than why) human beings get the results they do.

NLP originated at the University of Santa Cruz in the mid-seventies when a group of talented people led by Richard Bandler, John Grinder, and Frank Pucelik came together to share information and insights across disciplinary boundaries. It incorporates insights from behavioural and Gestalt psychology, family therapy, hypnosis, linguistics, information theory and anthropology, among many other disciplines.

Unlike some other schools of psychology, which concentrate on *why* problems arise, NLP started from studying people who are exceptionally good at what they do, and finding out *how* they do it so that anyone can get similar results by doing the same things. It aims to move beyond remedial change (fixing specific problems) to 'generative' change, which empowers you to achieve more in every area of your life. Often people find that when they learn a new skill or make a breakthrough in one area of their life, problems in other areas seem to disappear or seem less important.

By studying how 'star performers' in every field achieve their results, the developers of NLP have built up a vast reservoir of knowledge about what works in every field of human endeavour. You can apply the knowledge resulting from this curiosity to help others, to become more successful in your work, or even to tap into your own hidden resources.

The insights of NLP are being successfully used in business, education, sales, sports psychology, and health care, as well as therapy, coaching and self-improvement.

Another difference between NLP and other approaches is that NLP concentrates on the *structure* of experience, rather than the *content*. How you think about something is at least as important as what you are thinking about. So, for example, if you remember a pleasant experience as a big, bright, moving picture, it will probably give you a much more powerful pleasant feeling than the same experience viewed as a small, dark, monochrome snapshot.

One of the things that often surprises people about NLP is the speed with which many problems can be resolved. Solving one's problems is all about learning - at the unconscious level, which is where it counts - and learning can happen very quickly.

Some Principles of NLP:

- People have their own model of the world, and what they do makes sense within that model

- Mind and body are one system

- People have all the inner resources they need to succeed (there are no unresourceful people, only unresourceful states they get into)

- There is no failure, only feedback (results that we can learn from)

INTRODUCTION

- I am in charge of my mind, and therefore my results

We can't say that these principles are 'true' (nor can we disprove them by experiment) – what we can safely say is that when you act *as if* they were true, you get better results, enjoy your life more, and will be better able to cope with any challenges you face.

To learn more about the principles or 'presuppositions' of NLP, get the first book in the *Practical NLP* series, *Practical NLP: How to use NLP principles to improve your life and work, even if you're not NLP trained.*

2 'DEEP STRUCTURE' AND 'SURFACE STRUCTURE'

First, let's consider the structure of language as NLP sees it. Have you ever struggled to put what you are feeling into words? Have you ever tried to convey some information that you know inside out, but had a hard time finding the right words to express it as precisely as you want, not leaving anything important out?

What's going on there is that you know what you want to say - in NLP terms, we would say that you have a 'rich internal representation' of it, in images, feelings and other sensory information as well as words and concepts. But to tell someone else about it, you need to translate that rich stew of sensory information into just words - and inevitably, some elements are going to get lost in translation.

The way NLP thinks of language is based on Noam Chomsky's Transformational Grammar. This is an academic model, but the basic elements we need to know about for our purposes are this: our internal representation of what we want to say is called the 'deep structure', and the words that actually come out of our mouths, or that we write in a report or an email, are called the 'surface structure'. In plain English, the deep structure is the full richness of what you mean to say, the surface structure is what you actually say.

To get from deep structure to surface structure, our unconscious minds use three processes of translation. We leave some information out - ***Deletions;*** we make ***Generalisations*** rather than describing every single time a similar event happened; and we make assumptions that can lead to ***Distortions***, where we unconsciously bend the facts to fit our beliefs, or we accidentally introduce distortions by using a word that could be ambiguous or misleading.

All of this happens unconsciously; we don't consciously select every word that comes out of our mouths, because it would take far too long to say anything. In fact, our unconscious mind is better at forming grammatical sentences that flow properly than our conscious mind is. Perhaps you have noticed times when you have put a lot of conscious thought into choosing exactly the right thing to say, and yet your words come out more stilted than usual?

'DEEP STRUCTURE' AND 'SURFACE STRUCTURE'

On the listener's or reader's side, the same processes of deletion, distortion and generalisation are also running, in order to translate the 'surface structure' of your words into the 'deep structure' of what the listener or reader ends up thinking that you meant. The listener fills in deleted gaps with information from their own map of the world - which may or may not be the same information that you left out. They filter the words through their own generalisations and introduce their own distortions. The end result of this filtering may be very different to what you meant to say.

Because we are running these translation processes of deletion, distortion and generalisation unconsciously, we are usually not aware of the deletions, distortions and generalisations that show up in our speech. Most people are never aware of them. But each time this distortion, deletion or generalisation happens, it leaves behind linguistic markers - evidence in the choice of words and the sentence structure that something has been deleted, distorted or generalised.

If you don't know how to spot these 'markers', it's more likely that you end up accepting the assumptions and generalisations embedded in what someone is saying without even realising it, even if you might not agree with those assumptions if you were consciously aware of that they were present.

Skilled communicators can *presuppose* certain things in their language to get people to see things from their point of view, or to frame an issue in the way that's going to benefit them (we will learn more about *presuppositions* in the next chapter). Unskilled communicators, on the other hand, often don't make their case as well as they might, or don't make themselves as clear as they could be, because they are not aware of the deletions, distortions and generalisations in what they say. The result is that they often don't get the results they want.

So which kind of communicator would you rather be - skilled or unskilled?

3 PRESUPPOSITIONS

Presuppositions are linguistic assumptions - in other words, what you have to accept as being true in order to understand what is being said. Pretty much everything you say, everything you hear, everything you read, has presuppositions in it, which influence the internal representations of the listener - or your internal representations if you are listening to someone else.

Presuppositions are useful for both *recognising* what is assumed by in what someone says, and for *creating internal representations* in the minds of your listeners or readers.

The previous book in this series, *Practical NLP: How to use NLP principles to improve your life and work, even if you're not NLP trained,* was about the "Presuppositions of NLP" - a set of ideas that you have to assume to be true, or least act *as if* they are true, in order to get

NLP to work for you. Those are specific examples of particular ideas being presupposed, not to be confused with the concept of presuppositions as a whole, which is what we are considering here.

Let's take a look at the different kinds of presuppositions that can show up in everyday language, and how to spot them. Being able to identify the presuppositions in a statement or question will enable you to read between the lines of what someone is saying, and give you information about their map of the world that the average person would miss.

This knowledge will also enable you, with practice, to be able to structure and sequence the internal representations of people you communicate with - whether you are managing, coaching, or informing them - so that you can get your message across, influence, or develop people in the most effective way.

Most people are not aware of how the presuppositions in their language impact the effectiveness of their message. Sometimes they will undermine what they want to say, without even realising it. As you practice and get better at using presuppositions with awareness and intention, you will find that your ability to get your message across, to influence people, to manage and develop people, gets better and better. Being aware of the presuppositions in your language, and being able to use them effectively, will make a massive difference to your ability to get results with NLP.

So, we've said that presuppositions are things that you have to assume are true in order to make sense of what the person is saying. But they're not explicitly stated in words. If someone says to you, "I only closed the deal on the fourth meeting", you instantly know how many meetings they've had, and that the deal wasn't closed in the first three. They don't have to explicitly say "I had four meetings and I didn't close the deal in the first three but I did in the fourth one." You know there were three previous meetings, because the word "fourth" *presupposes* that; it would make no sense to talk about the 'fourth meeting' unless there had been three meetings previously.

You've probably heard the saying that when you assume something, it makes an *ass* out of *u* and *me*. To get better results than that, we need to be able to distinguish between what is definitely presupposed in someone's statement, and assumptions that we might make that would lead us to interpret their statement in a certain way that isn't necessarily what they meant.

How do we recognise when presuppositions are being used? There are a number of different kinds, each with its own tip-off or 'linguistic marker' that alerts that the presupposition is there - let's briefly look at some examples for each kind so you can identify it easily.

Note: I first encountered the presuppositions as formulated here in through the work of the veteran NLP trainer Tad James. It draws from NLP co-founders Richard and John Grinder's list of 'Natural Language Presuppositions' (as presented in their book *The Structure of Magic Volume 1*), which they state borrows heavily from the work of Lauri Kartunnen.

Existence

The first kind of presupposition is the presupposition of existence, and the tip-off for it is the presence of nouns, or people, or places.

Here are some examples:

- The management noticed Richard's ability early on.

- The management only just noticed Richard's ability.

- The management didn't notice Richard's ability.

What's interesting about this is that each time you read one of those, you had to accept the idea of 'Richard's ability' in order to make sense of the sentence. I didn't even have to say 'Richard has this ability and the management noticed it early on'. Just mentioning the noun 'ability', almost in passing, while your attention was on Richard and the management, was enough to presuppose that it did in fact exist.

So presuppositions are able to create internal representations in the listener's mind (or put ideas in people's heads, as we would say in everyday English), while the conscious attention of the listener, and hence any resistance they might have to what the speaker is saying, is displaced elsewhere in the sentence.

Of course, if someone sits down and thinks about it, they could say 'Hang on, who says that he actually has this ability?' but more than likely their attention will be shifted to the other elements.

Notice also how it doesn't matter if there's a negative in the sentence - in order to make sense of 'They didn't notice Richard's ability', you still have to accept the existence of the ability, almost without thinking of it. Whether or not the sentence is positive or negative in nature, the effect of the presupposition is still the same.

Presuppositions of existence can be very useful in questions, especially open questions. If someone asks a closed question, "Have you had any benefits from studying this material so far?" you might answer "no", even if there have been lots of benefits but it's just taking you a while to think what they are. On the other hand, when you ask the open question "What benefits have you had from studying this material so far?" it presupposes that there have been some benefits, and it makes it easier for you to find them and bring them to your conscious attention. This is a very useful structure to remember if you're doing coaching, or if you're doing assessment or gathering feedback which at the same time can also embed learning or get customers to realise just how much they've got from your product or service.

Possibility or Necessity

The tip-off for presuppositions of possibility or necessity is the presence of 'modal operators'. Modal operators are words like *should, shouldn't, ought, got to, have to, must* - modal operators of necessity - or *can, can't, could, couldn't*, which are modal operators of possibility.

Here is an example: Sooner or later, Sarah needs to realise that she can close the deal.

There are two modal operators in that sentence - 'needs to' which is a modal operator of necessity - it must happen; and 'can', which implies possibility. You could just say to Sarah, "Sarah, you can close the deal" to which she could easily say "no I can't". If you say "When are you going to realise that you can close the deal?" her attention will be shifted to the question of when she's going to realise and she'll be more likely to accept that closing the deal is possible.

The great thing about presuppositions of possibility or necessity is that when you hear someone use those modal operators, they are giving you clues as to their beliefs and the rules they operate by - what they must do, what they mustn't do, what they should do even if they aren't doing it, and what they think is possible or impossible.

These rules are important, because they guide the person's behaviour. Very often the beliefs about what they should do, what they must do, or what they can't do, turn out to be false and limiting, and just holding them back. Whole schools of therapy have grown up around getting people to recognise and rethink their musts, shoulds, ought's, and can'ts. When you can hear those presuppositions in what someone is saying, you can subtly use more empowering presuppositions, just in conversation and without making a big deal of it, to help them expand the limits of their mental maps.

When you hear a lot of shoulds, can'ts, 'got to's, and musts, that's usually a sign that the person is experiencing themselves as being at the 'effect' end of things rather than 'at cause' - they feel as if the world is operating on them rather than the other way round. One of the ways they keep that going is by the presuppositions in what they say to themselves in their internal dialogue, and which usually also show up in what they say out loud.

If you want to use a presupposition of possibility in a question, the format "How can we...?" or "How could we...?" is very useful to get people thinking and coming up with ideas. It presupposes that whatever comes after that question opening is in fact possible.

You can even use a presupposition of necessity in order to open up a sense of possibility: "What do we need to do to gain a share of this market?"

presupposes that it's possible to gain a share of the market, and will displace attention onto what we need to do rather than onto the question of "is it possible at all?"

Cause and Effect

The next type of presupposition is cause and effect. The tip-off for this is the verb 'to make' or 'to cause', or implied causatives of the form 'if-then', or just the word 'because'.

Cause and effect makes a linkage between two internal representations, labels one a cause and the other an effect, and says "this one causes that one", or "if you do this one, that will happen".

Examples:

'The tightening market made him up his game.'

'One of the reasons people select our service is because it gives them total control.'

'I don't know which aspect of the course will give you the biggest benefits...'

Again, notice how this still works even when you start with a negative:

'Don't sign up for this programme unless you are ready, because it will give you a lot more business.'

Here's an example with an 'if-then' structure:

'If you throw in the aircon, then I would consider buying it'

Other tip-off words that have essentially the same structure as if-then:

'*While* the market is in this state, I'm being very careful about where I put my money.'

'*As long as* you keep us as your exclusive supplier, we'll keep prices stable.'

'We won't take on any more people *unless* we get that big order.'

Complex Equivalence

This is another form of linkage that people make between different internal representations, and the tip-offs are the verb 'to be' in any form, or 'means'.

What we're doing with complex equivalence is either saying something *is the same as* another, different thing (hence the name) as in "Time is money" - or saying that something *means* something else, or is *a sign of* something else: "They've increased my salary, that means they really value me". Sometimes you get an implied complex equivalence; that last example would still mean the same if you said, "They've increased my salary, they must really value me" - because the 'that means' is understood.

Presuppositions of complex equivalence, when you hear them, give you clues about how people categorise and label the world around them. Also, you can use complex equivalence presuppositions to get people to make connections that they hadn't seen before, or assign new meanings to things: "If you're feeling confused right now, that means you're taking on board new information, which is part of the process of learning". Notice that although there's an 'if' in that sentence, it's not the same as the 'if-then' of cause and effect. In fact, we're saying that the feeling of confusion is actually an effect of the process of learning - which, if they accept it, redefines confusion in their mind as a good thing.

Awareness

The tip-off for these is any sensory verb - see, hear, feel, touch, smell, taste - or any neutral, non-sensory verb implying awareness, like 'notice', 'realise', or 'become aware of'.

"John could see the possibilities" - that's telling you that there are possibilities. Again, even if the sentence contains a negative ("John couldn't see the possibilities") you still have to accept the idea of possibilities in order to make sense of the sentence.

If you want to use this presupposition in a question, you could say, "Have you noticed what's happened?" which presupposes that something has happened. Or "Which benefits have stood out most for you?" implies that there are benefits, and even that there may be some that you haven't noticed yet because they've been overshadowed by the more prominent ones.

I don't know if you've noticed yet how this presupposition is actually a subset of presuppositions of Existence - but using awareness verbs to imply the existence of something is so common, and so useful, that it's worth giving Awareness a category of its own.

Time

Presuppositions of time place an event or an action before, after or during some other events or time periods, and can be used to imply a sequence of events. The tip-off is verb tenses, or time-related words like 'when', 'stop', 'start', 'until', 'now', or 'yet'.

Examples: this is a useful one for an aftersales or technical support situation, if someone comes to you with a problem. You could say to them "I understand you're having some problems with the product". Although this is an accurate description of the situation, it's not the best way to describe it if you want the customer to feel more hopeful, because the '-ing' in 'having' implies something ongoing. You could say "I understand you **had** some problems with the product" which puts the problems in the past - but that may not fit with the customer's experience, as they're probably experiencing the problems as still going on, and they might feel like you're trying to claim that everything's OK now.

So you could say "I understand that you've **been having** some problems." That still fits the client's experience - the problems may have been occurring right up to this point - but it also places the experience in the past, and opens up the possibility that we can fix the problems from now on.

Let's look at 'stop' and 'start'. Just stop - and notice how much you've learned so far. When you tell people to stop, that's what they tend to do - they stop doing everything, including thinking, at least for a moment, so it's a good idea to follow that immediately with what you want them to do.

"When did you stop sabotaging yourself?" presupposes that there was a time when you were sabotaging yourself, but that time is now over. "Have you started to realise your potential?" implies that there was a time when you weren't realising your potential - and that time may or may not be over. "When will you start to realise your potential?" definitely says that you haven't yet, but suggests that you can.

We can get interesting results if we use a Time presupposition in combination with a presupposition of Awareness. "You may not have realised yet how much you've learned" presupposes that the realisation will happen, and of course that the listener has learned something.

Adverb/Adjective

The tip-off for this is an *adverb* or *adjective*. If you're a little shaky on the distinction between these terms, here's an easy definition: an adjective modifies a noun, while an adverb modifies a verb.

So the *adjective* 'easy' in 'easy definition' leads you to expect that what follows will be easy to understand, and it probably is easier than if we just said 'this is the definition', if only because you won't be telling yourself 'this is going to be hard'. 'Easy' and 'hard' are both adjectives. See how they change the way your internal representation of whatever noun they're applied to? If I say 'here's the important thing about adjectives', that pretty much ensures that you'll pay more attention to it than the rest of the presentation. Interestingly, the important thing about both adjectives and adverbs is that you already use both of them expertly, even if you didn't know that's what they were called.

Now, fortunately, when you put an *adverb* at the start of a sentence, it places a frame around what you're going to say that tells people how to receive that information. Here are three examples of exactly the same information, but using different adverbs to put different frames around it. Notice how each one would be received:

'Unfortunately, sales were unchanged this year.' Oh no! It's terrible! No increase in sales!

'Fortunately, sales were unchanged this year.' Phew! What a relief! We must have been expecting them to go down - or that's what's implied by 'fortunately' anyway.

'Interestingly, sales were unchanged this year.' Well, yes, that is interesting. I wonder what caused that?

See how useful that could be?

Inclusive/Exclusive Or

The tip-off here, you won't be surprised to learn, is the word 'or'. So what's the difference between the 'inclusive' and 'exclusive' versions of this presupposition?

The 'exclusive or' offers a choice between alternatives but excludes all other possibilities. "You can do either *this* or *that*." Usually just two alternatives are offered, but there could be more: "Our choices are *this*, *that*, or *this third option*."

If you have kids and they are young enough, you can use exclusive ors to give them the illusion of choice while still doing what you want: 'Do you want to have your bath first, or tidy your room?' Of course, after a while they eventually catch on and say 'who says I have to do either?', but it's great while it lasts.

That pattern is known as a 'double bind'. The great hypnotherapist Milton Erickson used to use double binds a lot to give his clients choice about how they moved in the direction that Milton wanted them to. 'I don't know if you want to go into a trance now, or after a while, and whether you would like a deep trance or a lighter trance' - but they were going into trance whatever.

The double bind also the basis of the 'Alternative Close' in sales - 'Would you like it in red or black?' 'Will you be using cash or credit card?' which excludes the possibility that the customer won't buy at all, while including options of finish or how to pay. This pattern can work well, as long as the customer is at the right point in their buying cycle. Using the 'exclusive or' too early in their buying cycle would make the customer feel pressured, and you would lose rapport.

Another situation in which to be aware of 'exclusive or' presuppositions in your own language is if you're gathering customer or user requirements, or gathering information about a client's problem. You'll notice that 'Are you working with a large team, or a smaller one?' is a closed question - although it's not going for a yes or no answer, it's still giving the listener just two alternatives to choose from. It's forcing the conversation down a particular path, quite possibly in the direction of your preconceived notions of what the solution should be, which means you may be missing important information. Open questions that don't limit the alternatives on offer work much better.

Other words that exclude other possibilities are words like 'only', as in "Only you can decide" which excludes the possibility of me, or anyone else, trying to tell you what to choose; and 'just', as in 'Just focus on the essentials' which aims to exclude focusing on anything else.

The 'inclusive or' offers one or more choices, but also leaves open the possibility of other unspecified options: "We can do *this*, or *something else.*" It presupposes that other choices exist, and does not shut the door on them. The 'inclusive or' is useful in meetings, or a mentoring situation, when you have a suggestion, but you are open to other possibilities.

Ordinal

The final type of presupposition to consider is 'Ordinal', and the tip-off is words like 'first', 'second', 'third', or 'last', implying a position in a list.

Remember that example from near the beginning of this chapter, "I only closed the deal on the fourth meeting"? So that's presupposing that there were three meetings before that.

The word 'then' can also imply a list or sequence; "Find the right customers, then find out their needs, then tell them how you can meet those needs".

Ordinal presuppositions are great for coaches to embed learning, especially when combined with presuppositions of awareness. "It may not be until the third or fourth time it happens that you notice how much better you've become at asserting yourself" presupposes that even if you haven't noticed it yet, the positive change could already be happening.

'Presuppositions or assumptions' exercise

Let's try a couple of quick exercises in identifying the presuppositions in what people say.

1. Imagine someone said the following sentence to you:

    "I'm not sure whether or not I should stop fiddling my expense claims."

Now, here are some comments on that sentence, and your job is to identify whether they are presupposed in the sentence, or just assumptions that the commenter has made that aren't necessarily true.

a) **He is claiming expenses.** Presupposition, or unwarranted assumption? Take a moment to think about your answer...

   ... It's presupposed in the sentence. It would make no sense to say "my expense claims" if the person could not claim expenses. Actually, just to show that presuppositions are everywhere, that comment contains another presupposition, which is what? ...

   ... Yes, 'he' presupposes that the speaker is male.

b) **He doesn't like his job.** Presupposition, or assumption?

... It's an assumption. The sentence says nothing about how he feels about his job, and we would be jumping to conclusions if we decided he didn't like it. In NLP, by the way, this pattern of making assumptions about what someone is thinking or feeling is called a 'mind read', and you will have noticed that people do it all the time (extra points if you spotted that 'you will have noticed' is also an example of a 'mind read').

c) **He currently fiddles his expenses.** Presupposition, or assumption?

... It makes no sense to talk about stopping fiddling expenses unless the speaker is already doing it, so that presupposes that the fiddling is already going on.

d) **He is an indecisive character.** Presupposition, or assumption?

... It would be jumping to conclusions to decide that his whole character is indecisive on the basis of one example. He might be ultra-decisive in every other area of his life - so it's just an assumption.

Now some examples for you to try for yourself, with no answers given so you have to make your own judgments. I should warn you that just as in real life, some of these not as straightforward as they might appear at first sight.

2. "I don't see why I can't do it. All my colleagues are doing it!"

   Which of the following would be jumping to conclusions, and which are presupposed in the statement?

   a) **She feels that management is treating her unfairly.**

   b) **She wants to be accepted by her colleagues.**

   c) **Her colleagues do something she is not currently doing.**

   d) **Because her colleagues are doing it, she wants to do it too.**

3. "If I don't learn how to assert myself, I won't get promoted."

   a) **He blames himself for his lack of promotion.**

   b) **He doesn't know how to communicate with his superiors.**

   c) **He wants to learn new behaviours.**

   d) **His salary is connected to his communication skills.**

How confident are you in your answers?

4 THE HIERARCHY OF IDEAS ('CHUNKING')

Now that you understand presuppositions, it's time to consider another important aspect of language - the 'Hierarchy of Ideas'. This is to do with how abstract or specific your language is, which of course indicates where on the spectrum between overall big picture and fine-grained detail your mind is focusing. This is also known in NLP as 'chunking', because our minds seem to process information in a small number of 'chunks', and people vary as to how detailed or big-picture the amount of information held in each 'chunk' is; and sometimes as 'levels of abstraction', because the higher up the Hierarchy of Ideas you go, the more abstract the concepts you are dealing with. This will become clear when we look at the example later in this chapter.

Being aware of the Hierarchy of Ideas is important, because the more flexibly you can move up and down the levels of abstraction, the more successful you will tend to be in work terms, and the more skilled you will be at dealing with people who are stuck at one end or the other of the detail/big picture spectrum. As an executive coach, I've found that one of the main reasons that stop people from being promoted to director level is not being able to think strategically - in other words, they haven't been comfortable thinking at an abstract level, which is what top-level leaders are required to do. The higher up the organisation you are operating, the more you have to think in terms of the big picture.

From time to time, you may have had to work with someone who is a real nitpicker. If you ask this person to do something, they need you to tell them exactly how to do it, down to the finest detail; or maybe they go and do it, and then they come back and tell you the entire story, step by step, of how they did it. If you ask this person how their weekend was, they'll tell you in excruciating detail and chronological order each thing they did. And if you interrupt them, they feel they have to start the whole narrative again from the beginning!

Alternatively, you may also have worked with someone who only thinks in big-picture terms, and is bored by details. They only want to know the overview, or what's important, and they will do their best to avoid practicalities. They'll give you vague instructions, and if you ask them about how you want them to do what they're asking, it's a real struggle to get them to come down to some kind of practical level.

What you have there is two people at opposite ends of the NLP metaprogram called Chunk Size, or General/Specific. If you're detail-oriented yourself, you'll be asking at this point 'What's an NLP metaprogram?' If you're more at the big picture end of the spectrum, you'll be confident that you'll be able to pick up the meaning from the context.

'Metaprograms' in NLP are usually defined as something like 'the content-free filters we use to sort information'. In practice, they are a number of patterns that describe what we focus our attention on. There were about 60 of them when Leslie Cameron Bandler and others originally identified them back in the early days of NLP, and usually nowadays most NLP trainers teach a more manageable 14 or so of the most useful ones.

Metaprograms, by the way, are usually taught in depth at NLP 'Master Practitioner' level, but this one is worth mentioning here because it is very relevant in a business context, and also quite easy to get your head round.

So, General/Specific, also called 'Chunk Size', is one of the most important metaprograms in NLP. The idea is that rather like a computer, our minds have a certain amount of working memory that we use to hold whatever we are thinking about at any given time. Space in our working memory is quite limited, so we are only able to process a small number of chunks of information at any given time. This is often rather inaccurately quoted as 7±2, following psychologist George Miller's research in the 1950s, but more recent research, as well as everyday experience, suggests that in practice we have more like 3 or 4 chunks of information available in working memory.

So how do we investigate something in more detail, or zoom out to see more of the bigger picture? We change the amount of information in the chunks. We can 'chunk up' to a bigger chunk size, or 'chunk down' to finer levels of detail.

Let's see how to do this in practice. Have a look at this Hierarchy of Ideas diagram, with the box called 'Motorcycles'. How many makes of bike can you name?

The Hierarchy of Ideas

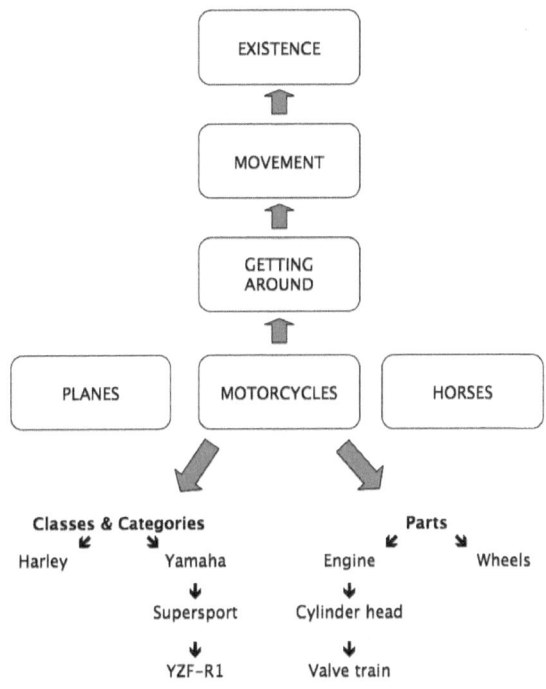

Some people are not that interested in bikes, and just see them as something that other people have, and they can probably name Harley-Davidson and two or three others. A real bike fanatic, on the other hand, will know all the makes including defunct ones like Vincent and BSA, and would then be able to reel off all the names of different models from each manufacturer.

So one way you can chunk down from a particular category or class (like motorbikes) is to ask 'What are examples of this?' Naming a specific make of bike is more detailed than the class of bikes in general, and going down to specific models within a make is a smaller chunk size still.

Notice how the further down you chunk, and the finer level of detail you get into, the more scope for disagreement there is. Two people may both love bikes, but if you get them talking about their favourite bike and why it's so great, then they'll probably choose different models and have plenty to disagree about.

Also notice how there are different ways of dividing bikes into classes. You could distinguish between different manufacturers, or you could divide them into dirt bikes, cruisers, racers and so on.

Another way of chunking down, if you're starting at the level of individual objects rather than abstractions or classes, is to analyse the parts that the object is made of. My knowledge of bikes chunks down about as far as the engine, and doesn't get any more specific than that, so if I had one and the engine developed a fault I would have to take it to a mechanic who knows all of the engine parts and how they work together, and with any luck can trace the fault right down to the specific part that's malfunctioned. So the question to chunk down from the engine in general would be "What part of the engine?"

Let's look at chunking up to get to the big picture, or what's really important. Questions you can use to chunk up from the category of 'bikes' are: "What's this an example of?" Well, bikes are an example of a way of getting around.

Incidentally, you will notice that there are other categories of transport at the same level of abstraction, like buses, planes, boats, or horses. So we can also chunk sideways to one of those other categories by first going up one level, to 'ways of getting around', and then asking "What's another way of getting around?" We do this unconsciously all the time; going up one, two or even three levels and coming down in a different place is one way that we get new ideas, and get out of being stuck in problems.

If you want to keep chunking up, just keep asking the question "What is this an example of?" So what is 'getting around' an example of? One answer might be Movement. And what is Movement an example of? Existence - which is pretty much as abstract as it gets.

Other ways of chunking up are to ask, "What is this part of?" or with actions "For what purpose?" or "What's important about this?" which chunks up to the *intention* or *value* that's driving the action.

Now just as the more detailed you get, the easier it is to find things to disagree about, the easier it is to agree as you chunk up higher. Why? Because chunking up makes it easier for people to remember the broad principles that they are in agreement about, rather than getting lost in nitpicking details. So if you're in a negotiation or chairing a meeting and it's getting bogged down in disagreements about specifics, it's useful to chunk up to a higher level and remind people of the purpose of the meeting, or what is important to both sides in the negotiation.

Also, abstractions can mean different things to different people, because they don't have specific sensory referents to point to ('sensory referents' are things in the real world that you can see, hear or touch). Sometimes this is OK, but at other times it can cause problems as you get down into practical implementation, as the different interpretations of what people thought they were agreeing to come to light. Everyone is probably in favour of better productivity, but does 'productivity' mean 'the same people being able to produce more', or 'producing the same amount but with a smaller number of people required'?

At the abstract level, then, it can sometimes be useful to explore a person's grasp of the meaning of an abstraction by asking another 'chunking down' question like "What does this mean?" or "What will this mean in practice?"

THE HIERARCHY OF IDEAS ('CHUNKING')

Here is one more important thing about the effect of abstraction. Because abstract concepts are vague, and not physical real-world things that you can form a sensory internal representation of, when you hear or read an abstraction-word (like *quality*, *agreement*, remuneration, *morale* or *relationship*) you have to go inside and form your own meaning of it, either by finding a metaphorical image that symbolises the abstract concept, or events that (for you) are examples of it.

What internal representations do you form when you hear the word 'love'? Or 'personal development'? Probably each reader will have a different image, drawn from your own experience, or if you had no direct experience of the concept, what you imagine it to be like or what you have heard from other people. In effect, this puts you into a trance state; you're paying attention to what's going on inside your mind, rather than what's going on around you.

The first person to notice this effect was probably the great hypnotherapist Milton Erickson. Up until then, hypnosis had been about swinging watches and direct suggestions that you were getting sleepy. Erickson found that by talking to people 'artfully vague' language, with a lot of abstractions, he could get them to drift off into a trance state without using direct suggestions. This was very useful in his work, because it meant he could bypass any resistance his clients might have had to a more direct approach.

Have you ever had to sit through a long speech, maybe at a meeting or a company get-together, where the speaker is using a lot of abstractions, and you have found yourself drifting off and thinking about something else? That's exactly the same experience - except that unlike that speaker, Erickson knew what he was doing and was using the abstractions with intention, to aim your thoughts in directions that would benefit you.

There is another benefit in using abstractions in helping people to change. When Erickson talked to people about their inner resources, or about certain learnings they had gained, without specifying what those resources and learnings were, it allowed their unconscious minds to select the resources and learnings that were right for them at that moment.

So, as we said, a person will have a particular range of levels in the hierarchy of ideas that they feel at ease in. Some people will have quite a narrow band that they feel comfortable in - a person with a strong detail focus could feel overwhelmed by vagueness if you ask them to consider the higher levels of abstraction, while a person who only operates at big-picture level will get bored and frustrated at the detail level and think of it as nit-picking.

If you think about hierarchical organisations like the armed forces, people at the bottom of that hierarchy are given very specific tasks - "theirs not to reason why". As they rise through the ranks, each promotion involves handling higher and higher levels of abstraction, until at the level of the top generals and field marshals they are dealing with very high-level strategy. The higher the level of abstraction you can be comfortable with, the higher you can go in an organisation and the more you'll be rewarded.

Here's another thing to consider. Higher levels of abstraction are more powerful than lower levels of detail, and give you more leverage, because the higher level includes the lower levels. If you have a motivating value that's important to you such as achievement, for example, the many different things you could do to fulfill that value are at a lower, more specific, more concrete level. But they're all included within that abstraction of achievement.

That gives you an almost infinite number of choices for how to achieve that value. If one way is denied you, or it has downsides that make it not worth going for, you have choices about other ways to achieve that value. But someone bogged down at the more concrete level may be stuck with just one way of achieving the value. If that way is denied them, they won't easily be able to change what they are doing to find another way of fulfilling the value. So if circumstances change, as they do a lot these days, they won't have the adaptability to succeed.

Being able to handle higher levels of abstraction, then, gives you more leverage and more flexibility. In today's environment where we have to deal with increasing amounts of complex, uncertain, ambiguous information, the ability to chunk up to higher levels of abstraction is increasingly valuable. Other things being equal, and as long as you also have what we can call emotional intelligence or people skills, that ability will get you promoted faster and more highly rewarded.

One of my teachers, Tad James, told a story about how he was making this point on an NLP course and a student at the back stuck his hand up and said "Hang on a minute - I'm a philosophy postgrad at the university, I deal in very high level abstractions all day long, and I get paid an absolute pittance!" And Tad pointed out that what actually gets you promoted or rewarded highly is the ability not just to operate at the big picture or strategic level, but also having the flexibility to be able to move down to more specific levels and communicate what that means in practice to people who are operating at those levels. So flexibility, and getting comfortable with chunking up, down, or sideways as needed, is the key. Live NLP trainings generally include some practical exercises to develop that flexibility.

Review

So far we've been playing with deep structure and surface structure in language, presuppositions including existence, possibility and necessity, cause and effect, complex equivalences, awareness, time, adjective/adverb presuppositions, exclusive and inclusive or, and ordinal. And we've just been scampering up and down the hierarchy of ideas, chunking up, down and sideways.

So I wonder how you're going to be using presuppositions to make your communication and influencing skills more effective?

And I also wonder at what levels of abstraction in the Hierarchy of Ideas you find yourself most comfortable, and what benefits you'll see when you get more flexible and comfortable in dealing with abstractions, ambiguity and uncertainty.

5 THE META MODEL

In this chapter we explore the set of magic questions called the 'Meta Model', which help you to uncover missing information, challenge generalisations, and straighten out distortions. The Meta Model is going to be ultra-useful to you in all kinds of contexts: therapy, coaching, business, and not least in your own personal development and aspects of everyday life, like parenting and spotting the tricks that politicians and sales people employ to get their own way.

So bearing in mind the Hierarchy of Ideas from the previous chapter, you'll remember that 'chunking up' takes us to a more abstract level and into the realm of concepts and ideas that could mean different things to different people, while 'chunking down' takes us to a more specific level, to concrete things and actions that we can compare with our sensory experience of things and actions in the world around us. This chapter is all about how we chunk down to get more specific, using a set of questions called the Meta Model.

Origins of the Meta Model

The Meta Model was the first model created by the originators of NLP, Richard Bandler and John Grinder (*modelling* in NLP deserves a whole book to itself. It is essentially the process of taking on the skills of another person through replicating everything they do - behaviour, thought processes, beliefs and body language - and then stripping out everything that's not needed to get the results, the end product being a *model* of how to reproduce that skill that can be transferred to other people). The Meta Model patterns were originally modelled from the questions that two great therapists, the family therapist Virginia Satir, and Fritz Perls, the father of Gestalt Therapy, would ask their clients when they heard signs in their language that they were operating from some distorted beliefs, or making sweeping generalisations, or leaving out some important information.

What and Grinder found was that by using these Meta Model questions, Satir and Perls could - in the nicest possible way in Satir's case and somewhat more directly in Perl's case - cut through the distortions, deletions and generalisations in what their clients said, and get to the real issues at the heart of their problems. Getting more specific enabled the clients to compare the problematic areas of their maps of the world (the parts that said 'here be dragons' or were just white spaces) with their own sensory experience.

Often the clients realised that the beliefs they had been operating from for years, unexamined, actually were no longer true; that there had been examples of them being able to do things that they thought they couldn't, or that there were exceptions to sweeping generalisations like 'I don't deserve success' or that 'I am just an unlucky person'.

Bandler and Grinder realised that, although Perls and Satir were very different people, and the content and tone of their interactions with their clients were very different, the underlying structures of the questions they asked were very similar. When they took what the two therapists' patterns of questioning had in common, and left out what was individual to one or the other, what they had left was essentially a field guide to how to spot language patterns that indicate distortions, generalisations and deletions, plus questions to reconnect each of those patterns with the facts of the client's sensory experience, that could be used by all therapists to get better results more quickly, whatever school of therapy they'd been trained in. So they called it the 'Meta' Model - 'meta' meaning 'over and above' or 'about'. Their guidebook to using the Meta Model is *The Structure of Magic, Volume I*, which I highly recommend you read if you are at all interested in the nuts and bolts of effective questioning.

So you might be thinking, "I'm not a therapist, how is this going to be useful to me?"

Knowing the Meta Model patterns and being able to ask precision questions in the right places can help you to:

- be alert to missing or unclear information

- get clarification on requirements, instructions, and what people expect of you.

- iron out misunderstandings

- get more and better quality information

- *really* sharpen your coaching skills

- and not least, be able to challenge limitations when they show up in your internal dialogue to expand and enrich your own map of the world, so that you have more choices.

Distortions

We can group the elements of the Meta Model into Distortions, Generalisations, and Deletions. In a coaching or therapy context you are usually going to get the most leverage by going for the Distortions first, because they hold the biggest chunk size of information. In business situations, where you're not necessarily trying to change someone's beliefs but just communicate in the way that will get you your outcome, which questions you ask first will depend on the context.

Let's run through the Distortions first.

1. Mind Reading

If you are doing a presentation to a prospective client, and the client says "I know you're just trying to manipulate us into buying something we don't need", how do you change her mind? In that situation many people might just deny the charge, but that probably won't work - the more you deny it, the more the client may think you are trying to manipulate her. So what do you do instead?

Let's be clear about what's happening here. The client is speaking as if she definitely knows your intentions, or your thoughts, or your emotional state. In NLP we call this "mind reading".

What recognising this pattern gives you is an opportunity to find out more about how the client is thinking, so instead of protesting your innocence, you could ask, "If you don't mind me asking, what gave you that idea?" What we really want to know is "How do you know?" but we're softening it a little to maintain rapport. In answering that question, the client will give you more information about her belief systems and how her map of the world operates.

2. Value Judgments (or 'Lost Performatives' in the NLP jargon)

Another distortion that we humans introduce is putting things into categories, such as: good or bad, useful or useless, great or terrible, effective or ineffective, helpful or harmful.

Why is that a distortion? Well, those categories are not there in the physical world; they are subjective evaluations that our mind makes, based on our own values and prejudices. Which means, of course, that some people will make different evaluations than we do. Is the music of Barry Manilow great, or awful? The answer depends on whom you ask.

But people often pronounce these judgments as if they are absolute objective truth, forgetting that judgments are always a matter of opinion. If we knew what standards they were using to judge, we might agree with them, or we might not; at least we would understand how they arrived at that judgment, and might be able to present new evidence to change their minds.

Notice that judgments like 'brilliant' or 'hopeless' are just opposite ends of a spectrum, and there are all kinds of shades in between. When people are in a strong emotional state, those nuances disappear; they might say "He is a hopeless salesman" or "She is a terrible manager" when a cooler, more objective assessment might place the person being judged

THE META MODEL

nearer the middle of the spectrum. Value judgments matter, because they become part of your mental filters, and can influence the views of other people. If it becomes generally accepted that "she is a hopeless manager", anything good in her performance is probably going to be screened out by confirmation bias.

So the question that you might ask yourself when you hear a value judgment is "By what standard are you judging?" or "How has this judgment been arrived at?" Those questions get the speaker to look again at the evidence criteria for their judgment, and may perhaps open the possibility of change. Notice the way that "How has this judgment been arrived at?" is less personal and so less challenging than "How have you arrived at this judgment?" so that's the form I would go for in most cases.

The standard response question you will see in most NLP books to a value judgment is "Who says?" or "According to whom?" Remember that Bandler and Grinder originally modelled these patterns from a therapy context. Therapy clients sometimes inherited value judgments from their parents that they had never really examined, just parroting them as if they were universal truths. They didn't say, "My father always said that I was good for nothing", they just said "I'm good for nothing" - the original 'performer' of the judgment had been lost from their statement.

I must say that even in a therapy context, whenever I've asked that "Who says?" or "According to whom?" question, the client usually thinks for a bit and says, "Well, according to me!" So I've found "By what standard are we making this judgment?" to be a much more useful question, and even more so in a business context.

In a therapy context, reflecting back or paraphrasing the belief statement in a way that invites the person to take responsibility for it can be helpful: "So you're saying that you're good for nothing?" This can form a platform for further investigations or challenges; for example, in *Richard Bandler's Guide To Trance-formation* he follows up the "So you're saying that" paraphrase by asking the client the client "How do you know that?" - inviting the client to re-examine the belief against sensory experience.

3. Cause and Effect

We have met the cause and effect relationship before in presuppositions, and the tip-off words are exactly the same: the verb 'to make', or other words that mean the same thing. Essentially this is a sign that someone is not 'at cause'.

People will sometimes say things like "He makes me angry", or "She upset me", or "That woman's bangles clicking as she types are driving me nuts." They feel, for that moment at least, like the 'locus of control' is outside of them, and other people or external events are responsible for the way they feel. Since the cause is outside of them, in their map of the world they can't do anything to change it, so they feel powerless and stressed.

In coaching for anger management, where people seek help because they don't have much control over their impulses, you get client statements like "I had to hit him... because he looked at me." The emotional reaction and the behavioural response are so automatic that the person feels as if what the other person did *caused* their action.

So if we were coaching that person, or even challenging our own internal dialogue if we say things like that to ourselves, what could we ask that could widen the gap between the stimulus of the external event and the response?

Try this: "How did that external event cause you to respond in that way?" - or more simply, "How does A cause B?" Answering that question will get people to examine their own processing, and maybe realise that they do have some choices.

This cause and effect pattern doesn't just crop up in a personal development or therapy context. It shows up in a work or business context where alternative responses have been ruled out, or have never been considered: "Market conditions have *forced* us to cut back production" or "We won't be trying anything new *until* sales improve."

In effect, the speakers have narrowed down their focus to one little bit of their map of the world, possibly excluding other viable choices that are available in other parts of their map.

Again, answering the question "How has *this* caused *that?*" can get the person to re-examine how they got to the conclusion that this is the only choice, and maybe get them to consider some other options that they had missed.

Notice how the cause and effect relationship is sometimes presupposed rather than explicit: "We won't do B *until* A happens", "*As long as* A, then B", "*While* A is true, we will do B". Sometimes that implicit cause and effect is worth questioning, to open up more choices: "How is B dependent on A?" or "What's the relationship between B and A?"

4. Complex Equivalence

Remember our mind-read example, where a prospective client says "I know you're just trying to manipulate us into buying something we don't need" and we ask, "What gave you that idea?" or "How do you know?"

In answer to that question, the prospective client might say: "As soon as you started using that NLP jargon, I knew I couldn't trust you." Now first of all, you would never find yourself in this situation, because why would you use NLP jargon with anyone who isn't trained in NLP? But more importantly, they're giving you an insight into their thought processes. In their minds, there's an equivalence that says something like "NLP is manipulative", or "Using NLP jargon means this person is trying to bamboozle me". Complex equivalences usually come out in the form "A is the same as B" or "A means B" - where A and B are two different things. The giveaway is the word 'is' or the word 'means' - though sometimes in the real world, as in the example of "As soon as you started using that NLP jargon, I knew I couldn't trust you" they don't make it easy for you by resolving it into exactly that format.

By the way, if you question a mind-read, the answer will usually come as some form of complex equivalence. One question usually won't clear everything up - you listen to their response, check for any Meta Model patterns, and use an appropriate question in response.

The question that should be occurring to you here is "How is A equivalent to B?" or "How does A mean B?" So in this case "How does using NLP jargon mean you can't trust me?" Of course you probably wouldn't ask it straight out like that - you would add softeners like "If you don't mind me asking..." or "Help me out here, I need you to explain..." or just not ask the question out loud at all, but just file it away as useful information about the person.

What this pattern gives you when you hear it is an idea of how this person categorises things, or the meaning they place on particular events - in other words, how some bit of their map of the world is put together. If someone says "Time is money", they're telling you pretty much all you need to know about their attitude to time.

People's complex equivalences are set up by experiences they've had at different points in their lives, by what they've been taught, and people they've met, books they've read, even films and TV shows they've seen that have made a big impact on them.

In the context of relationships, you can get problems when people have different complex equivalences. If one person in the relationship might be thinking "He never brings me flowers, he doesn't love me"; to the other person, love might mean keeping them safe and working hard to put food on the table. Love is a 'nominalisation', an abstraction, and there are many different ways of expressing it. Flower, chocolates, romantic cards to one person; protecting and providing to another person. So people in a romantic relationship need to find out what the complex equivalences for being loved are for their 'significant other', and make sure that from time to time they remember to do the things that make that person feel loved.

The same principle applies for working relationships. I used to have a boss who was a big fan of the bestselling business book *The One Minute Manager*. When he wanted to show me I'd done something well, he used to pat me on the shoulder and say "Well done!" Unfortunately, for me, getting that from him was a complex equivalence for being patronised. So if you want to show your colleagues or direct reports that you value them in a way that's meaningful to them, you need to find out what their complex equivalences for being valued are, rather than just using your own and hoping they will work. How will you know if it is working? Pay attention to the other person's response.

5. Presuppositions

You already know about presuppositions from the previous chapter. So if you hear an example like "Don't cause any more difficulties", the question "Hang on - who says I've caused any difficulties? What difficulties am I supposed to have caused?" will automatically occur to you. If you get a sales person asking you "Do you want to pay by cash or card?" before you're ready to buy, of course you will raise a question like "Who says I want to pay?"

A catch-all question for any type of presupposition is "How do you know <whatever the presupposition is>?"

Distortions Review

So to sum up this section of the Meta Model, these are the Distortions, with suggestions for how you might question them (if that's appropriate).

- **Mind-reads** such as "I know you don't like me" for which the question would be "How do you know that?"

- **Value judgments** or 'lost performatives' such as "This is the best model on the market?" for which the question would be "How has that judgment been arrived at? By what criteria are you making that judgment?"

- **Cause and effect** statements like "He makes me angry" for which the question is of the form "How does he make you angry?"

- **Complex equivalences** like "A is B" or "A means B", for which the question is "How is A the same as B?" or "How does A mean B?"

- **Presuppositions**, where you can ask "How do you know <whatever the presupposition is>?"

If you want a quick and dirty way of remembering the appropriate questions to use for distortions, notice that you can use "How?" questions for all of them.

Generalisations

As the name suggests, generalisations are either sweeping statements that say 'all examples of this are the same' or 'this has never happened', or else unquestioned rules about what should or shouldn't happen, or what you can and can't do. This reflects black-and-white thinking and inflexibility; a person who uses a lot of generalisations is not going to be very comfortable with uncertainty or ambiguity (most of the time anyway).

We all use generalisations as a set of general guidelines for finding our way around the world; if we had to think every decision out from first principles, it would take a very long time to get anything done. Most of the time they work OK for us; sometimes, these generalisations hold us back, or get in the way of seeing opportunities, or - as in the case of racial or gender stereotyping - cause problems for other people as well. So it's useful to have some questions ready for when we need to challenge generalisations in our own internal dialogue, or we want to get other people to re-examine their own prejudices.

6. Universals ('Universal Quantifiers' in the NLP jargon)

Universals are what we would normally think of as generalisations in everyday English. "Everyone does it", "It's never going to happen", "Things always go wrong for me". The tip-off words include 'all', 'nobody', 'everyone', 'always', 'never'.

Of course, we may also hear more positive generalisations such as "It's all good", but usually we don't need to challenge these.

Interestingly, you can also get sweeping generalisations without any tip-off words being explicitly stated, like "Sales people are manipulative" or "Bosses grind you down."

When people make universal generalisations like this, they're not considering any possible counter-examples - either because they've heard the generalisation so many times that they just repeat it without thinking, or because they are in the grip of such a strong emotion that at that moment that they've forgotten about the counter-examples and the generalisation just feels true at that moment.

So we need a question that might get them to notice counter examples. One way you can do this is just to repeat the universal in a questioning tone - "Nobody? Ever?"

Or you could ask "Has there ever been a time when this wasn't the case?"

A potential problem with these 'standard' questions is that they can seem confrontational, especially if used insensitively. At the very least, they will feel like a challenge to the belief expressed in the statement, which may make the person defensive.

THE META MODEL

What a therapist or coach is wanting to do with a 'universal' statement like "This always happens" is to get their client to compare the generalisation to their actual experience, and so to recognise that actually the generalisation is not universally true. Once some exceptions are found, it opens up a 'possibility space' where the client might be able to make the exceptions happen more often. This is less likely to happen if the client feels pushed into defending their limiting belief.

A better question would do the same job (of looking for exceptions) without provoking a defence. The question is more likely to do this if it starts from the client's 'map of the world' and 'paces' (goes along with) the implied belief on the surface, while also getting them to look for exceptions to the generalisation.

So here's a question that does just that. It came up in an NLP therapy discussion group on Facebook, and was contributed by a rising star of NLP, Duff McDuffee. Duff's a very bright guy, and his scientificgoals.com website has made me update my approach to goal-setting, even though I've written an acclaimed book on the subject.

Duff said that when he gets a client who says something like "It's always bad" or even just "Things are terrible" (which kind of implies a generalisation because it ignores any silver linings or moments when things might be better), he often uses the question "When is it worse?"

When is it worse? What a great question. Why? Because it 'paces' (goes along with) the client's generally negative world-view so it doesn't break rapport, and *at the same time* implies that there is some variation in how bad things are.

As with anything in human affairs, there's going to be variation in a problem – sometimes it's worse, sometimes it's better, as this question tacitly reminds the client.

Of course, you don't want to spend very long on the bad stuff, because the longer the client talks about how bad their life is, the more they're going to associate into it and feel worse. So you'd spend just enough time on it for the client to recognise that there is some variability in their situation.

Note that if Duff had used a more traditionally solution-focused question, like "When is it better?" he would risk losing rapport with the client. It might be too much of an effort for the client to shift 180° from focusing on the negatives in the situation in the space of one question.

Instead, the question takes the client's view of the situation smoothly from "100% terrible" to something with more light and shade. From there, it's an easy next step to start asking about the times when it's not so bad.

7. Modal Operators

OK, back to the jargon! 'Modal operators' are words which indicate that there's a rule, like 'should', 'ought', 'got to', 'have to', 'need to', 'must' - these are called 'modal operators of necessity', or that indicate that something can or can't be done - usually 'can' or 'can't' - which are called 'modal operators of possibility'.

Let's take modal operators of necessity first. If someone says "I have to do it", or "I must do it" that suggests that they don't have a choice - which is inherently a stressful way of thinking by the way. If they say "I should do it" or "I ought to do it", they're giving themselves a hard time for not doing it.

Now you could ask "Who says you have to do it?" - that would send them back looking for the origins of that rule, and wouldn't necessarily be the most effective question; what if they don't remember, or if they came up with that rule themselves as a result of their interpretation of their life experiences?

It's generally more effective to ask questions about the consequences, because the way that people keep limiting rules going is often to imagine terrible but unspecified consequences. So when someone says "I must do this" you can ask "What will happen if you don't?"

That question gets them to look at the possible effects of the option they have been ruling out. They may realise that actually this option isn't so bad as they thought, and they do have a choice; or at the very least, their answer will give you more information about their map of the world.

So if someone says "I must do it" and that prompts the question "What will happen if you don't?", what might you ask if someone says "I mustn't do it"? How about "What will happen if you do?" Again, this looks to the consequences.

With "should" and "ought", you could ask "What stops you?" I'm not that keen on this question, although you see it in many NLP books, because it focuses people on negatives and they may start coming up with more reasons to justify the rule. I find that "What will happen if you don't?" and even "What will happen if you do?" will get you more high-quality information.

With modal operators of possibility, you generally aren't going to want to question statements where people say "I can" - unless it's something like "Yeah, I can do brain surgery" in which case I'd probably be asking things like "How do you know?" and "Could you unstrap me from this table please?" The beliefs that limit people are usually expressed as "I can't" rather than "I can".

When people say "I can't do something" they generally mean "I can't do it *yet*", because they haven't yet learned how, or gained enough experience to believe that they can, or "I *don't want to* do it" because either it goes against their values or they think there's too much effort involved.

To question an "I can't" statement, you could ask "What stops you?" which might be the right question in some cases - you can help them to identify the steps involved to be able to do it. You can also ask, "What would happen if you did?" If there is anything holding them back from wanting to do it, this question will usually uncover that constraint, or maybe strengthen their desire to do it because they get a better sense of the benefits that will come from taking that action.

So any time you hear a modal operator of either type that you want to challenge or find out more about, "What will happen if...?" is a good question.

Generalisations Review

To sum up this section, here are the Meta Model Generalisations again:

- **Universals** or 'Universal Quantifiers' such as "Nobody likes me" or "It happens every time", for which the questions would be "Nobody? Every time?" or "Has there ever been a time when it didn't happen?" (looking for exceptions to the generalisation); or more subtly (if we want to look for variations, opening the way to recognising exceptions, while maintaining rapport with the person), "Which people like you most and least?" or "When does it happen more often?"

- **Modal Operators**: of *impossibility* - "I can't do it", of *necessity* - "He ought to leave me alone", "I must get my homework finished", and of *possibility* - "I can leave whenever I want".

 The most elegant way to challenge the limitations indicated by modal operators is usually to ask "What would happen if you did/didn't?", "What if he doesn't?"

Deletions

'Deletions' are where the speaker has left some information out. If that information is important, either because it's holding the person back in some way, or because you need that information in order to do what they are asking you to do, you're going to want to ask questions to recover what is missing.

8. Nominalisations

'Nominalisations' are processes that we talk about as if they were things, verbs that we've turned into nouns. So 'communication' is a nominalisation - it's been made into a noun so we can talk about it as if it's a thing, but actually it's a process. So is 'love', so is 'rapport', so is 'business', 'work', and at a bigger chunk level words like 'the economy' and 'the market'. In real life these are not static objects, they are processes - people doing stuff.

So when we turn a process into a thing, we're deleting the activity in the process and 'freezing' it into an abstract concept. That obviously loses a lot of information, which can cause problems in various ways.

The first way it can cause problems in communication is that your listener may not know what the nominalisation means. A lot of nominalisations are long words derived from Latin or Greek, and if a listener hasn't been educated in that area, they might not understand what you mean. The term 'nominalisation' is an example; it means 'the process of turning a verb into a noun' and it's not widely known outside of linguistics and NLP. John Grinder's books are full of nominalisations derived from linguistics and logic that you don't see every day, and it's best to keep the dictionary handy when you're reading them. The question "What does that mean?" is a useful one here.

Another problem in communication is that nominalisations can mean different things to different people, because of the loss of information that happens when you 'freeze' the verb into a noun. You may be reasonably clear about how you decide something, but when someone talks about a decision that they made, they're not giving you any information about the process they went through to make that decision. So if it's relevant, you may want to ask a 'denominalising' question, that turns the noun back into a verb and restores the steps of the process, like "How did you decide?"

If someone is just talking about a decision, they are not even including the quite possibly relevant information of *who* it was that decided.

Because you lose the details of the process, nominalisations become abstract concepts rather than anything you can form a mental picture of. You can form an internal representation of talking to someone, but 'communication' or even 'conversation' are vaguer, less punchy, less vivid. You have to go inside to find an example of those concepts, rather than being able to form sensory images straight away.

So if you really want what you say or what you write to sparkle, don't use a lot of nominalisations - you won't hold the attention of your audience as well as if you use juicy, sensual words that can leap out and grab your listener's imagination. This is worth watching out for, especially if you've got a strong 'Ad' preference ('Ad' standing for 'Auditory digital', another bit of NLP jargon meaning that you prefer to think and process information through internal dialogue rather than using visual images, sounds or feelings) or you work in a business environment that encourages Ad expressions.

Aside from the obvious disadvantages of potentially not being understood and sending your audience to sleep, nominalisations can set up limiting ways of seeing the world. If someone says "I'm in a bad relationship", it sounds like the relationship is something outside of them that they have no control over. What they are really describing is the process of them relating badly to the other person. So if you ask a question that 'denominalises' that statement like "How are you relating badly to that other person?", it gives them an opportunity to re-examine what they have actually been doing that's led to the bad result, and maybe change it.

Another feature of nominalisations is that they lend themselves to the passive voice, which has a distancing effect. If a company's management says "The decision was arrived at to terminate your employment", what they mean is "We decided to terminate your employment." When you turn the process of deciding into the nominalisation 'Decision', it becomes a thing and the speaker can distance him- or herself from what they have done. If you want to recover some of the missing information, you could ask "Who decided that, and how did they decide?"

9. Unspecified Verbs

These are simply verbs that aren't as specific or clear as you need them to be. If your boss puts you in charge of a department and tells you "I want you to turn this department around", you might want to ask "How specifically?" If you don't get that information, you would have to fill in the detail of how to do it from your own map of the world - which might be very different from the boss's map.

All verbs are unspecified to some extent, and people would soon get fed up of being asked "How specifically?" when they ask you to do something. So it's a judgment call about when you ask the clarifying question - you only ask when you actually need the missing information.

10. Simple Deletions

We can identify a statement as having one or more 'simple deletions' if information that you need is left out altogether. If someone says "I'm more upset than I've ever been!" you would want to ask the question "About what?"

You would only want to ask the question if you need the missing information. Many things that that we say have some simple deletions, and sometimes it's not important to know what that information is.

11. Unspecified Nouns ('Unspecified Referential Index' in the NLP jargon)

This is where it's not clear which people or what things the speaker is talking about. "It's going well" – what is? "Certain people aren't pulling their weight" –

which people? Who specifically? Again, you would only ask the question if you need to know the answer.

12. Comparative Deletions

With this final pattern, there is a comparison being made, but the speaker is not saying what the comparison is with. People use this one all the time:

"This is the best model on the market". Better than what? And, come to that, better in what way, and in what markets?

"That's a lot of money." Compared to what?

So your question, if you need to ask one, will aim to recover information about the missing other side of the comparison.

Deletions Review

These are the Deletions in the Meta Model:

- **Nominalisations**, which are processes that we talk about as if they were things: 'a decision' rather than the process of deciding, 'a relationship' instead of the process of relating. To recover the information left out in the process of 'freezing' the process into a thing, consider asking "What does <nominalisation> mean?" or if possible ask a question that turns the noun back into a verb: "How did you decide that?" "How were you relating to that person?"

- **Unspecified Verbs,** where it's not clear how the verb was or is to be carried out: "I want you to improve quality." If you need to, ask how or how specifically this can be done.

- **Simple Deletions,** where a word or phrase is left out of the statement completely: "I am much encouraged!" If it's important, ask "About what?" or whatever appropriate question will recover the missing information.

- **Unspecified Nouns** (or 'Unspecified Referential Index'), where it's not clear what or who is being referred to. This is usually indicated by pronouns ("*They* won't let me get ahead") or constructions like "*Certain people* aren't pulling their weight" or "*Some of* the dogs are causing trouble". If you need to, ask "Who specifically?", "Which people?", or "Which dogs exactly?"

- **Comparative Deletions** such as "It's better that way" or "Things have got worse". Better than what? Worse than what?

Using The Meta Model In Practice

If you read some NLP books, you'll see Meta Model language patterns like "He upset me" or "Everyone's doing it", referred to as "Meta Model violations", and the questions linked to each pattern as "challenges".

This actually isn't a very helpful way to think of them, at least not if you want to maintain rapport.

Questions from the Meta Model, or any kind of "challenging" question, need to be used with care if you don't want to wreak havoc on your working relationships. A reader of my *Practical NLP* blog sent in a question about how to use Meta Model type questions which is worth quoting (he's kindly given me permission to do that):

"I was recently posed a question by an employee stating that something "Always" happened. I knew that it didn't happen all the time and when I replied by returning the question 'Always?' I was told by my peers that I was being aggressive and not adopting a coaching approach.

How should I have dealt with the question without closing the conversation and without sounding patronising?"

What my correspondent did there was use one of the standard responses recommended by the NLP Meta Model for 'challenging' universals, or 'universal quantifiers'. The difficulty with using these standard responses is that it's not just a matter of delivering the 'challenge'; so much depends on how, and the context within which, you deliver them.

That 'always' is an example of what is referred to in many books on NLP as a 'Meta Model violation'. The very term 'violation' suggests something that is wrong, to which a 'Meta Model challenge' would be appropriate. Even if you don't intend it, the bald use of a response such as 'Always??' may be received as aggressive or patronising, and consequently damage the relationship.

There's an 'early days of NLP' story (which may or may not be true) about John Grinder teaching the Meta Model to his Linguistics class at the University of Santa Cruz, quite soon after he and Richard Bandler had come up with the model. The students went out buzzing - they couldn't wait to try out these amazingly precise questions and start uncovering the missing information and thought patterns that underlay the 'surface structure' of what people said.

The following week they shuffled back into the classroom looking like they've been through hell. They looked tired, scruffy, depressed; some of them had obviously slept in their clothes, others had been crying, and one or two had black eyes. Grinder asked them what had happened. "Well," said one, "I tried out some Meta Model patterns on my girlfriend, she was getting more and more pissed off, and after about half an hour she kicked me out of the apartment." Every student had a similar tale of woe – "I had a stand-up fight with my best buddy", "My family have disowned me", "My dog bit me" and so on.

That's what the Meta Model questions will do if you use them without regard to maintaining rapport. Nobody likes being interrogated. Here's how to use these very powerful questions to make your life easier rather than harder:

THE META MODEL

1. Use the Meta Model as a guide to recognising particular language patterns that indicate missing information, over-generalisation, or 'distorted thinking'. Have the appropriate response question flag up in your mind. But *choose whether or not you actually say it out loud*. Sometimes you may want to let the 'violation' go, or just bear it in mind as something to return to later.

2. If you do decide to 'challenge' the 'violation' with a question, don't ask the question in a challenging way. Use whatever 'softeners' you need to keep the relationship on track.

   Sometimes it's enough to just deliver the question in a softened, or humorous, tone of voice. Other times, you may want to ask the question in a different way, with some verbal 'softeners' around it. For example:

   "So, I'm wondering if there's ever been any times when there are exceptions – when something different happens?"

   Or "I wonder if you'd mind me asking..." or "Maybe you could tell me if there've ever been any times..."

   Or you could use a 'reflecting back' statement which will be taken as you checking your understanding, while at the same time posing the question in a non-threatening way: "So what I think you're saying is, this happens every single time, and there have never been any exceptions?" which you could follow up with "Are there any circumstances in which it doesn't happen?"

Again, you could soften these still further by adding "Let me just check my understanding..."

Or with the follow-up, you could say "Could there be any circumstances in which it wouldn't happen?" which is hypothetical and unthreatening.

3. Make sure that the "paralanguage" or non-verbal component of your conversation is right. In particular, your voice tone is important as it's one of the ways that other people use to tell how you are feeling, and hence how your question is meant. How you stand or sit in relation to the other person is important too. You don't want to be so close to them that you're invading their personal space, getting "in their face" about the issue.

Rather than facing them head-on (which is what the word 'confrontation' literally means) and across a desk (which could be interpreted as "keep your distance" or "I'm nervous of you so I will keep this barrier between us"), ideally you want to be standing beside them at a comfortable distance, so that you are 'facing' the issue together.

These kind of considerations would apply to using any kind of "challenging" question. Remember, your long-term relationship with the person is at least as important, if not more so, than retrieving any specific example of missing information or exposing a particular misconception in their thinking.

That's the Meta Model. If you need to chunk down to a lower logical level and get more specific on something – 'drill down' as they say – these are the questions you would use. Depending on what distortions, generalisations and deletions you hear, you would use these questions to get people to compare the distortions in their map with actual evidence; to challenge generalisations by looking for counterexamples; and to recover missing information that's been deleted from the statement, to minimise misunderstandings.

6 THE MILTON MODEL

In the previous chapter we learned the Meta Model questions for getting more specific and for, if you will, 'challenging' vagueness.

Now it's time to go the other way - communicating at higher level, vaguer, more abstract levels of the Hierarchy of Ideas so that you can talk directly to your listener's unconscious mind, as well as their conscious minds - and influence them at the unconscious level.

The set of language patterns we're going to use to do this is called the 'Milton Model', because Richard Bandler and John Grinder modelled them from the great 20th Century hypnotherapist Milton Erickson, the father of indirect suggestion.

Now you might be thinking "I'm using NLP in a work and business context, so why would I be interested in something modelled from a therapist, especially a hypnotherapist, however much of a genius he was?"

This is why: whatever area of business you're in, and whatever your job role, you can actually learn a lot from a therapist, especially a hypnotherapist, because there is one thing that therapists are very good at, if they know what they are doing. And that is influencing people to change their behaviour. When you get down to it, that's what a therapist does. When I was a hypnotherapist, people came to me wanting one thing - to change their behaviour, and change it fast. Whether that behaviour was smoking, or eating too much, or having unwanted emotional responses like phobias, they all wanted to change their behaviour.

So if you want to influence people in any way - to get them to buy your product or service, or to motivate your team, or influence your employer to see that you're ready to move up to the next level, or even if you are a parent and you're telling stories to get your kids to go to sleep, and you want to do this effectively, rather than the hard way of trying to do it all through their conscious minds, you need to know about this stuff.

Now another question that may occur to you is: is it ethical to influence people through their unconscious minds? Can I actually do this, especially in business? I've got news for you - you're already doing it.

THE MILTON MODEL

Everyone uses these patterns all the time, but most people don't know they're doing it, so they get unpredictable results and don't realise the effects they're having.

How can that be? Think about this: you cannot *not* communicate. I'll say it again, because it's important: you cannot *not* communicate. Everything you say is communicating. In fact you could even say that everything you say is a hypnotic suggestion, to the extent that it structures and sequences internal representations in the listener's mind. Even if you don't say anything, that's still a communication; imagine if you held a meeting with someone and then didn't say a word throughout.

So people who don't know about Milton Model patterns are like unskilled amateur hypnotists, influencing people and placing suggestions in their minds by accident without realising it, quite often influencing their listeners or readers in unhelpful directions.

You don't have a choice about whether you communicate or influence people, so it's worth knowing the Milton Model patterns so you can influence people with intention and know what you are doing.

Origins of the Milton Model

So what is the Milton Model, and what's so special about it? When Richard Bandler and John Grinder discovered the Meta Model, they thought they'd found the holy grail of change work. Questions you can ask that get people to see how their distortions, deletions and generalisations match up with the specifics of their actual experience? Fantastic!

Then they went to see Erickson and observed him working with people, and they found they were into a whole different way of looking at the world. Instead of asking questions to get his clients to be more specific, Erickson was deliberately using vague language to take his clients off into trance! He was actually using language patterns that the Meta Model classed as 'violations' - and the clients were benefiting!

What he was doing, at a very big-chunk level, was using artfully vague language to get his clients' unconscious minds to access their inner resources. The unconscious mind decided the specifics of what those resources were, because Milton believed that your unconscious mind knows best what's right for you, even if it sometimes needs a bit of help to find that knowledge.

Some readers might still be thinking, "Well, I'm not a hypnotherapist, and I have no interest in being able to put people into trances and have them accept anything I say to them, or even in having ways of having their unconscious minds access their inner resources to solve problems. So why do I need to know about the Milton Model?"

Here's the important thing: if you ever want to change the way people feel, or influence them in any way, even if it's just getting your kids to calm down or cheer up a colleague, to the extent that you've had success in doing that, you've almost certainly been using some of the Milton Model already, without realising it. If you want to convey your belief in someone who works for you or that you're teaching, if you want to raise the morale of your team, if you want to paint a picture in a customer's mind so they can see the possibilities, you're going to find it hard to do that without using the Milton Model.

And when you do use it, and practice it, with immediate results but getting better and better as you study it and master it, you will find that you become more effective at putting ideas across, and changing people's minds, in a way that honours their values. You're not controlling them - because, long-term at least, that just isn't possible - you're effectively communicating with them in a way that helps them to see the possibilities, become aware of the information they need, and achieve their outcomes in ways that dovetail with your outcomes and benefit both of you.

So with the Meta Model we've seen distortions, generalisations and deletions in language patterns as signs of limitations and limiting beliefs. In the Milton

Model we see how you can use those exact same patterns for a different purpose, just slotting in different content or different words, to help people get past their limitations, and to motivate and influence them in a particular direction that works for them.

Distortions

Mind Reads

I know you remember from the Meta Model chapter that 'mind reading' in NLP is when someone is speaking as if they know what's going on in the mind of the listener. In the Milton Model we turn that idea round: just by saying that you know what's in someone's mind, you can put the idea or feeling or even action that you're talking about into their head.

I expect you're wondering 'how does that work?' - and if you weren't wondering before, you probably are now. And *you could be thinking* 'how can I use this in real life?' And right about now, I know that you're thinking of ways that you can use mind reads in real life, and pretty soon you're going to have a couple of ideas for how this pattern can put ideas in your listener's mind.

Lost Performatives

Or can we just say 'value judgments'? It's good if we do. 'Lost performatives' are value judgments where person who originated the judgment is left out and the judgment is just presented as a fact. And it's OK to do that most of the time, and even better when you spot someone doing it.

You can use lost performatives to validate the way someone is feeling or what they're doing - "It's a good thing to feel comfortable" - which encourages them to do more of it. Or you could use it to 'pace' something that your audience is feeling, or that might even be an 'objection' in the broadest sense of the word, before suggesting a direction out of it: "It's natural to feel a bit confused at this point, before you decide the best thing is to just accept it and go with it." (Note: 'Pacing' is another type of Milton Model pattern that will be explained a little further on in this chapter.)

Cause and Effect

What is the relevance of cause and effect linkages to influencing? If you ask people to do something, their minds automatically demand a reason, and mostly they won't move on until you give them a reason. Now here's the interesting thing: it's not that important if the reason makes sense, as long as there is a reason.

Research backs this up. The famous 'Xerox Study' by social psychologist Ellen Langer went like this:

There's a Xerox machine - a photocopier - in a library with a long queue of people waiting to use it.

You go to the head of the queue and say "Excuse me, I have 5 pages. May I use the Xerox machine because I'm in a rush?"

What proportion of people would let you in, do you think?

According to the study it was nearly everyone - 94%.

They repeated the experiment lots of times in different libraries. They also tried this different wording:

"Excuse me, I have 5 pages. May I use the Xerox machine?"

What proportion would let you in now?

This time it was only 60%. So what was the difference? The reason or cause: 'because I'm in a rush'.

Finally, they tried this wording:

"Excuse me, I have 5 pages. May I use the Xerox machine because I have to make some copies?" So you've given a reason for jumping the queue, but it's not a valid one, since everyone queuing for the photocopier presumably has to make some copies.

Would you care to take a guess at what proportion would let you in with this wording? The answer turned out to be 93%!

So the difference between giving a valid reason and giving a reason that's not valid is just one percent - and either one is over 30% more persuasive than not giving a reason at all. Our minds seem to be searching for cause and effect linkages, and once they see that structure, they're not so bothered about whether the cause is really responsible for the effect.

If you get your head around the power of cause and effect linkages, then you're well on the way to becoming a master of influence. So the 'if-then' structure that I employed in the preceding sentence is another cause and effect pattern you could use. Notice how it works equally well if you leave the 'then' out, because your mind, once it sees the 'if', will take the 'then' as understood. If you understand that, you're well on your way.

You can use other words than 'if' - "*Once* you realise that, you'll be a master of influence". We are still saying that realising that point will cause you to be a master of influence.

The if-then construction works equally well in the negative: "*Until* you realise that, you'll *never* be a master of influence."

And there are other words like "*As long as* A, then B" and "*While* A, then B" which you can use to imply a cause and effect relationship between A and B. "As you read this chapter, your unconscious mind is storing away these language patterns for later use."

You can also imply cause and effect using a negative and the word 'unless': "Don't take the time to practice using these patterns unless you want a dramatic increase in your power to influence people".

Here's one more format, which goes 'the more A, the more B' or 'the more A, the less C': "The more times you re-read this book, the more you'll find yourself wanting to try out the Milton Model in real life." The more you practice, the easier it gets. Or - the more you use the Milton Model, the less resistance you'll meet.

That's a very common pattern, and now that you've heard it, you'll spot it all over the place. (That last sentence was yet another version of the cause and effect pattern, by the way).

Complex Equivalence

You will remember that Complex Equivalences take the form 'this *is* that' or 'this *means* that'. You're saying that something is the same as something else, or that it's a sign of something else. Did you remember that's what Complex Equivalences are? If you did, that's a tribute to your persistence. And if you didn't, that means you need to read the Meta Model chapter a couple more times.

When you link two different things as a complex equivalence, you get the listener to look at the first thing in a different way. People sometimes get confused when they start learning NLP, because it's such a different way of looking at things. Confusion just means your mind is taking in new information, before it's fully integrated. In fact, confusion is a natural step in learning - right before understanding.

Do you need any more examples? Reading this book *means that* you're committed to your own development. Or in a sales context, "The fact that you're here *means* you're serious about buying."

Presuppositions

Remember, presuppositions are what you have to assume to be true in order to make sense of what's being said. Have a look at the following examples.

Here's a great question you can use in problem-solving:

"Where is the problem on a scale of one to 10, where one is the worst it's ever been and 10 is where you're going to be when you've solved the problem"

What's presupposed there?

That you're going to solve the problem.

"When you've told me what you need, we'll be clearer about how I can help"

There are two presuppositions in that one: you're going to tell me what you need, and there is some way that I can help.

So that's the Distortions part of the Milton Model - Mind-reads, Value Judgments, Cause and effect, Complex equivalences, and Presuppositions. These are the same patterns as in the Meta Model, but you're just using them in a different way.

Generalisations

Universal Quantifiers

Every reader, or nearly every reader, will remember from the Meta Model chapter that these are words like *all*, *every*, *no-one*, *always*, *never*, and so on.

You should use these with care in business. Not *everyone* in business is a critical thinker, so they won't *always* pick up on sweeping generalisations. I don't even have to say "sometimes they might" because using universals with a negative already implies that some of the time, sweeping generalisations will get noticed.

You can also use universals with predictions to create desired internal representations of 'what-if' scenarios in the listener's mind: "One day soon, every business will have one of these" sounds more likely than "What if every business had one of these?"

Finally, you can use universals in a presuppositional way: "Everything you've learned since you've been doing this job" doesn't specify what exactly has been learned, but allows the listener to find the most relevant or important examples, because it presupposes that there definitely are some. This is especially useful where you are coaching someone or just want to talk to your colleagues or your team in a way that increases their confidence.

Modal Operators

As you might recall from the Meta Model chapter, these are words we use when we are implying rules or making statements about possibilities or impossibilities. They point to the existence of generalisations about what should or could be done. Like all human beliefs, they are not necessarily true, but they point the listener's thinking in certain directions, useful ones if you employ them skillfully.

There are two kinds of modal operators: modal operators of necessity, which are words like *should*, *oughts*, *must*, *have to*, *got to*, plus the negative versions like s*houldn't* and *mustn't*.

Some examples of how you could use modal operators in an influencing context:

"Sooner or later, a person has to wake up."

"You don't have to put this into practice straight away - unless you want to see a big improvement in your results."

And when you use modal operators with any kind of action words, like "We've got to make this happen today" they add intensity and gee people up.

The other kind - modal operators of possibility - can be used to suggest possibility, as in "We can do this" or "There could be a way round it." This can help to boost morale or to open up new ways of thinking and new ways round a problem.

Deletions

The following patterns are classed as 'Deletions' because some information has been left out, which of course leaves a gap that the listener has to fill in from their own map of the world.

Nominalisations

By now you will be in *possession* of the *knowledge* that these are *processes* or *activities* that have been turned into nouns. So the process of succeeding is turned into 'success', the process of deciding becomes 'a decision'. You will notice that in order for the process to be turned into a thing, a huge amount of information is left out - such as who's doing the deciding, how they decide, how long it takes, and so on. This is why we can class nominalisations under 'Deletions'.

Nominalisations are used a huge amount in business, and often in a careless way. They are great for using as a shorthand way of describing complex processes - like 'business development' or 'organisational change' - as long as both communicator and listener have a shared understanding, and you are aware that the nominalisation is leaving information out.

In *consequence*, they're best used where the subject matter demands a high level of abstraction, or where you want people to find their own examples - "as you consider your successes in the past year" or "when you look at your most effective decisions, you'll find certain commonalities".

Because nominalisations turn actions into objects, they also have the effect of - literally - getting the listener to look the situation more objectively, and of reducing the emotional temperature. "That's the decision" sounds more immovable and at the same time less confrontational than "That's what I decided".

The downside of overusing nominalisations is that they don't form clear internal representations in the listener's mind, so using too many will sound vague, slippery, or boring - plus there is the possibility of misunderstanding if the listener finds examples that aren't the ones you want.

Unspecified Verbs

These are the antidote to micromanaging. When someone is experienced in their job and getting good results, you don't need to tell them exactly how to do each step in detail - they already know that. In fact, they may know better than you, as it's their job.

So you can tell them what you want them to do, without getting too specific about how they do it. "How about we grow this account by 50% this year?" or "I'd like you to get comfortable with the new system." You are not telling them how to grow the account or get comfortable with the new system.

Unspecified verbs are also good for setting a direction for people's thinking, for example in sales, although you will then have to give some specifics to back up the implied claim: "Buying this system will transform your business" - and then you can go on to make clear how it will do that.

Finally, unspecified verbs are great for encouraging creative thinking, especially when combined with modal operators of possibility: "How can we increase sales?" "What could help to streamline the process?"

Simple Deletions

Simple deletions can be very useful. What for? Well, I could leave you to fill that gap that I left with your own ideas, but I'll also suggest a couple of examples.

Simple deletions are good for inspiring: "We're well on the way" doesn't say where to, but it sounds good. "If you're happy, we'll move on" doesn't say what they're happy about, or where we're moving on to - but often you don't need to.

We all use simple deletions a lot - otherwise it would take forever to say anything. As ever, you need to pay attention. "What to?" you may be wondering, as I left that bit out? The answer is: your listeners. Make sure, by calibrating their responses, that they haven't misunderstood, or that they don't need more context or detail than you've given them.

Unspecified Nouns ('Unspecified Referential Index')

"It's going well, isn't it?" What's going well? I'm hoping that you'll take the 'it' to refer to your growing understanding of the Milton Model; some people get it straight away, and some people enjoy a bit of confusion before it all falls into place. Which people? I don't need to specify - and actually, it's fine to be in either category.

When you think about some of the insights you've had while you've been learning about the Milton Model, I wonder what possibilities for useful applications you can see, and what opportunities for improving some aspects of your communication you've already identified?

Notice how that last sentence didn't specify what the insights were, what the possibilities were, what applications you can see, what the opportunities were, and which aspects of your communication you want to improve? I didn't need to - because you will already have found your own examples of each. In fact, I didn't want to specify 'communication' either, because for certain people (there we go again) it will be written communication, for others it will be verbal, and maybe some of you are communicating through graphics or through actions, and that's what sprang to mind for you.

Comparative Deletions

Comparative deletions are where you make a comparison, but you don't say what to... leaving the listener to fill in the gap from their own map of the world.

"The company is now stronger" - stronger than what? The competition? Stronger than it was before? Maybe both. You can let people take their own meanings from the statement. Sometimes it's *better* that way, and you will be a *more effective* communicator for it.

You can also link two comparative deletions. We've already seen cause and effect linkages - "The more you practice, the better you get" - and you can also use two comparatives when you want people to stop doing one thing and start doing another: "A little less conversation, a little more action" in the words of Elvis.

So that's the first part of the Milton Model, and as you can see it consists of language patterns that are the same as the Meta Model. The only difference is in how we use them. We use the Meta Model to spot these patterns in other people's words, and identify the appropriate questions that we might want to ask to help the person compare their distortions, generalisations and deletions against their sensory experience.

In the Milton Model, we're using the exact same patterns deliberately to make it easy for the listener to detach from their sensory experience and go inside. Erickson used this for assisting people into a therapeutic trance; in business we can use it to bypass conscious resistance and craft messages that tailor themselves to the listener's map of the world, because the listener is filling in the deletions in the surface structure of our words from their own map.

We are also using the Milton Model to frame what we're saying, so that the listener pays more attention to what we want them to notice, and less attention to whatever might get in the way. And finally, in coaching, we can use the Milton Model to help the person we are coaching to find their own inner resources.

Pacing

There is more to the Milton Model than just the Meta Model stood on its head. Bandler and Grinder also modelled other language patterns from the great hypnotherapist Milton Erickson, as well as particular ways of speaking that enabled him to communicate with his client's unconscious mind at a deep level, at the same time as the surface of his conversation was occupying their conscious mind. Read on to find out what these are.

This next set of patterns we can broadly describe as 'pacing'. If you've read anything about 'rapport' in NLP, you will remember that pacing is going along with or matching a person's current experience, to help them to feel comfortable and relax into a rhythm with you, and that can be a preliminary to then leading them somewhere that you want them to go.

Pacing Current Experience

This is simply describing the person's experience in a way that is undeniable, so that they have to agree with it. The effect of pacing current experience is relaxing - the part of a person's mind which scans their environment for trouble, or in a business setting, for things to mismatch and disagree with, is lulled to some extent by a sequence of three or four of these pacing statements.

"So you're reading this book, and you've come quite a way already, and we're now deep into the Milton Model, and you're already aware of how you could use certain patterns in practice..."

You will notice that we've just had a series of statements that must be true for the reader, followed by a mild suggestion.

'You're reading this book' - of course you are. If you weren't, you wouldn't be seeing those words.

'You've come quite a way already' - why, yes I have Andy!

'We're now deep into the Milton Model' - yes we are.

With the next statement - 'you're already aware of how you could use certain patterns in practice' - I'm actually departing from pacing statements and throwing in a bit of a suggestion. It's theoretically possible that someone could have been reading all this and not have thought of any ways to use the patterns in practice, but I'm willing to take that chance to nudge them in that direction. In any case, I know that you're smarter than that - because in most cases the effect will have been to draw your conscious attention to various ideas about using the Milton Model patterns that have been percolating away at the back of your mind.

Here's another example, that you could use in a meeting when you want to focus people's minds. "We're sitting here, in this meeting, and we're aware of how time's getting on, and we all want to reach a decision that works for everyone..."

We're definitely sitting here, and yes we're in a meeting. The next statement is a sort of self-fulfilling observation - they may not have been aware of how time is getting on, but they become aware of it as soon as you mention that they are aware of it. And the last bit - 'we all want to reach a decision that works for everyone' - is another sly suggestion. They may not all have been wanting to reach a decision that works for everyone, but tagging the suggestion onto the end of all that pacing will help to lead them in that direction.

Notice how in the first example, we linked the statements with 'and'. In the NLP jargon this is called a 'simple conjunction'. All this means is that it joins the statements together and makes the whole thing flow more smoothly. If you didn't use the 'and', the listener could just take them as a series of unrelated statements. The effect of the 'and' is to link them - it puts each statement next to the others in the listener's internal representation. Disagreeing with one of the statements would feel like rejecting all of the others as well - so since they agree with most of the statements, the listener's mind is more likely to let a mild suggestion pass without flagging up resistance. In the business context, spoken out loud, linking a series of statements with 'and' would be an unusual conjunction that might jar the listeners out of a relaxed and acquiescent state, so I omitted it.

Utilisation

This next pattern is just using whatever happens, or whatever the other person says - even if it's an objection, in a sales situation - to link to your suggestions and strengthen the points that you're making.

THE MILTON MODEL

The way Erickson employed utilisation was to use whatever happened to deepen his client's trance - even things that you would normally find distracting. So if there were people talking in the corridor outside his office, he could say to the client "any noises you might hear outside can just remind you how quiet it is inside". And I used that a lot when I was a hypnotherapist, or just when talking groups of people through a relaxation technique. It was great because you could get people to relax even in an environment that wasn't completely silent.

Or Erickson's client might say "I don't believe I'm hypnotised yet" and he would turn that into evidence that they were, by saying "That's right you don't... *believe*... you're hypnotised... because you're evaluating... being hypnotised... with your conscious mind and it's... you're unconscious... mind which knows how to be hypnotised now..."

We could spend a long time just unpacking all the different patterns in that statement, but this isn't a book about hypnosis. For now, let's just notice how he takes whatever they say and instead of disagreeing, runs with it - in the direction he wanted to go anyway. When he says "you don't...*believe*... you're hypnotised", on one level he's pacing their statement - he's using the exact same words - and, with a subtle emphasis on 'believe', he's also introducing a slightly different meaning: 'believe' in the sense of 'that's what you believe is happening, but actually you haven't noticed yet that there's something else going on'. The pauses, by the way, combined with the slow pace of his voice and its low, gravelly tonality, had a hypnotic effect on his clients. They rapidly learned that when Erickson spoke that way, it was time to relax and go into trance.

You could use a similar format to divert or overcome objections in a business context. If you are aiming to get your company to bring in a new system, and the objection is raised that "We're not ready for it", you could say "I agree - *we're* not ready" implying that the competition are.

For excellent examples of utilisation, look at how a good stand-up comedian deals with hecklers. The heckler *thinks* he's challenging the comedian; what he's actually doing is providing the comedian with an opportunity to generate more laughs.

Truisms

Truisms are generalisations which are undeniable - statements so obvious or self-evident as to hardly be worth mentioning - except of course that we use truisms all the time in regular conversation to set up the background for what we are going to say next, so it doesn't seem strange to your listener when you use them.

Examples would be 'sooner or later, you have to take a break'; 'most people work more effectively when they have ways of recharging their energy'; or 'a lot of the best creative ideas arrive out of nowhere'. There's not much to argue with in these statements, but they can preframe a suggestion or request that the listener might reject if you hit them with it without any preframing. "So would it be OK to experiment with taking a short break every 90 minutes, and monitor the results you get?"

Indirect Suggestions

Ambiguity

Ambiguity happens when a sentence has more than one meaning. When this happens, the conscious mind looks at the context to work out which meaning is correct, but the other meaning will still be registered by the unconscious mind. This isn't something I would overuse, and you certainly wouldn't want to be caught using it, but it's worth knowing about - not least so you don't unwittingly come out with random ambiguities that might create the wrong internal representations.

We can identify four kinds of ambiguity for indirect suggestions - the first is **phonological ambiguity**, where one word sounds like another. This is used a lot in humour, from - at the low end of the scale - puns, right up to the sublime heights of Ronnie Barker's "Four Candles" sketch. He asks for four candles, but it turns out he actually wants "'andles for forks".

The classic use of phonological ambiguity in sales is when someone says something like "You'll have heard all you need to **buy now**". I believe people are getting increasingly wise to this one, but you might get away with it if you deliver it subtly enough. In fact, if you were really sneaky, you could win a buyer's trust by quoting that to the customer as an example of the weaselly tricks that some sales people will try, while the 'you need two' that's also in the sentence sneaks past unnoticed.

Phonological ambiguity is also sometimes used in advertising slogans. "Coke refreshes you like no other can" - apparently this is an old Coca Cola slogan. Do they mean 'can' as in 'is able to', or 'can' as in a soft drink container? Both.

In **syntactic ambiguity,** the same sequence of words can be interpreted in different ways. There are at least three kinds.

The first kind happens when you add 'ing' to a verb and put it in front of a noun: "I don't like micro-managing managers" could mean two quite different things, depending on whether it's the speaker or the managers who are doing the micro-managing. Another example: "they are supplying businesses".

My own company is called "Coaching Leaders". Do we coach leaders, or are we leaders in coaching? Yes!

But note that this structure only works when both versions of the ambiguity make meaningful sense: "I like digging holes" wouldn't work because (as far as I have come across) there aren't holes that dig.

Another kind happens with the type of nominalisation where it's not clear who is performing the action or who it belongs to, as in: "the look of his eyes." Does this refer to how his eyes appear to others, or is it his eyes that are doing the looking? With "the journey of a lifetime", does that refer to a journey that stands out above all others in someone's life, or are we metaphorically referring to the lifetime as a journey?

A third kind of syntactic ambiguity is the kind that happens sometimes in newspaper headlines, and I include it just as something to be aware of so you don't say or write something that gets a laugh by mistake when you're titling a report or the subject line of an email. Headlines are especially prone to being misinterpreted because shorter words are left out to save space - so a Second World War headline read "Eighth Army Push Bottles Up German Rear" and another quoted by the Columbia Journalism Review read "Squad Helps Dog Bite Victim". Usually the ambiguity arises because some words can be read as either a verb or a noun, as with 'push' and 'bottles/bottles up' in the first example, and 'bite' in the second.

Scope ambiguity is where you can't be sure how much of a sentence a particular word or phrase applies to, so it sets up additional meanings in the listener's mind. So if you say "Speaking to you as a serious professional", does that 'serious professional' apply to your listener, or to you as the speaker? Both - so it would tend to boost your credibility to the listener and make them feel you are like them so as to build rapport.

This kind of scope ambiguity has been around for ever, but I first saw the structure unpacked by NLP copywriting expert Lou Larsen:

Speaking (or writing, or in some way reaching out) to you as a (compliment or quality they value)+(profession or the kind of person they see themselves as). More examples:

"Speaking to you as a concerned parent"

"Writing to you as a credible consultant"

and you can play with the word order:

"Appealing to you as a sales expert"

Here's another structure: "The dedicated staff and leadership" - who's dedicated? Just the staff, or does that cover the leadership as well?

Punctuation ambiguity is where it's not clear where one sentence ends and the next begins. Erickson could get away with a lot more of these when his clients were in trance, like "I want you to notice your hand me the glass". You might think this would be tricky to use in a business context. My good friend Jonathan Altfeld - check out his work at altfeld.com - came up with a particularly cheeky one along the lines of "only you can decide where to award the business... to me... there's only one way to go." If you naturally pause a lot when you're speaking, it's fairly easy to do. Jonathan can do it faster and it still comes out naturally, which must have taken a *lot* of practice.

If you like the sound of ambiguities, practice using them in safe situations - underdo it rather than overdo it - and see what you can get away with. And keep a notebook to capture your favourite examples of phonological, syntactic, scope and punctuation ambiguities.

What you can use will vary depending on your accent - I've heard American hypnotic inductions using 'interstate' and 'inner state'.

Embedded Suggestions

This next pattern is one of the most important ones for influence and getting people to do what you want them to do. To **create an embedded suggestion**, you can embed a word or phrase within the longer sentence that your listener's conscious mind hears, in a way that the unconscious mind hears the embedded suggestion even if the conscious mind doesn't.

Now actually, because **you're learning these patterns**, I want you to **notice embedded suggestions consciously** as well. Erickson used **to subtly mark out the embedded suggestions** - with a change of tone, or by pausing before each one, or with a significant look, or an emphasising gesture, or where it's appropriate **you could do it with a touch**.

This is called "analogue marking" - you mark out the words of the suggestions, which of course are in the 'auditory digital' modality, with a change in another channel - auditory tonal for pauses or changes of tone, visual for a look or a gesture, and kinesthetic if you were to use a touch. If you're familiar with the NLP 'Swish Pattern', you'll recognise the 'swisssh' noise in that pattern as another example of analogue marking.

Now when you **read this book more than once**, you'll see me **use all kinds of embedded suggestions**, including ones I'm not consciously aware of - my unconscious mind has been doing this for so long it can just **generate embedded suggestions easily**. I've used bold type to mark some of the suggestions I'm consciously aware of to make it easy for you to get started with spotting them.

Let's flag up some explicit examples of embedded suggestions:

"I don't know how soon you'll **begin to feel better**"

"When **you're ready to go ahead**, perhaps you can **give me a call**"

"What factors tell you when **it's time to buy**"

There's a subset of embedded suggestions called **'conversational postulates'**, where the suggestion or command is embedded in a yes/no question: "Are you able to **give me that order now?**" "Are you ready to **let me on the computer?**"

Technically, these are questions about their ability or readiness, and you would ask them when you know the answer is 'yes'. But really, you're asking for the order or for computer access.

I'm sure you can see that it's easy to embed suggestions in everyday conversation in such a way that you still make sense to the listener's conscious mind overall. My advice would be to underdo it rather than overdo it - even if you didn't emphasise the suggestions at all, the unconscious mind is still processing them, and you don't want to set off alarm bells with the conscious mind by appearing to speak oddly.

A Note on Intonation

Now, with the last few examples, like "What factors tell you when **it's time to buy**", the form of the words is a question, but I've marked out "it's time to buy" with a slight command tonality - my voice goes down at the end of the phrase - which turns it into a command.

So it's worth mentioning three types of intonation. Where the voice goes up at the end of the phrase, in English that traditionally indicates a question. Where the voice stays level, that indicates a statement. And where the voice goes down, that indicates a command.

You understand this?

You understand this.

You **understand this**.

The rising intonation is a form of analogue marker that tells the listener's unconscious mind to pay attention, this is a question. The downward intonation is another analogue marker that says "pay attention, this is a command."

There are actually two ways in spoken English that you can tell whether what someone is saying is a question or not. One is that rising intonation, and the other is the syntax or word order. The most common question syntax, as you know, goes like this: "Would you like to include the optional extras?" or "Are you ready to try this out?" You put a question at the front - 'would you like to...' or 'are you ready to...' and follow it with the fact or action that you are inquiring about.

So when you use that question syntax with a command tonality, that's a powerful way of influencing people. Consciously, the word order tells them that they are hearing a question, but their unconscious mind also picks up on the command. "Would you like to **include the optional extras**" or "Are you ready to **try this out**."

Just to add a caveat about the 'high rising terminal', as the rising intonation is called. This is increasingly used by young people in the UK and US, and particularly in Australia, for statements and even commands as well as questions. If you find yourself using it a lot, you need to be aware that it also makes you sound uncertain and lacking authority in certain situations - for example, in presentations, and when you actually do want someone to do something.

I'd like you to notice what tonalities other people - and yourself - habitually use. I'd also like you to experiment with using subtle command tonalities with embedded suggestions and notice what effect it has on people.

Extended Quote

I learned about this pattern from my first teacher of NLP, who told me about the impact it had had on her when she first heard it from Tad James in California at the beginning of the nineties. Tad was telling his class a story about when he was apprenticed to Richard Bandler. Richard told him that he was teaching a class in California fifteen years ago, and one of the students told him that Milton Erickson could just say to someone *"Allow your unconscious mind to give you whatever you most need right now, because your unconscious mind has all the resources you will ever need"* - and it would.

Now, there's a lot going on in that pattern. Firstly, who is speaking here? On one level it's me telling you this, but I'm also reporting what my teacher said, and she's talking about a story that Tad told, and he's telling a story about Richard Bandler. And within that is a story that Bandler's telling about his class in Denver, and within that is the student's story about Milton Erickson. That's quite a few layers, so it's easy for the listener to lose track of who's speaking.

And of course whatever the unconscious mind hears, it applies to itself. By the way, this is one reason why people who insult and slag off others are usually pretty unhappy themselves - every time they call someone a bitch or an idiot, their unconscious mind is taking it on board as 'applying to self'.

So although this is Erickson saying *"your unconscious mind has all the resources you need"* to an unspecified person in a story, the listener's unconscious mind also applies that suggestion or statement to itself.

Plus, the listener might not accept that suggestion just from me, but when the person in the story is someone they admire or respect, they are more likely to just take it on board. I heard Richard Branson speak about business decisions once, and he said that when he's decided the time is right, he'll just say "Screw it let's do it".

Just to step outside of NLP for a moment, that's Professor Cialdini's "Authority Principle" in action. Cialdini's not an NLP guy, although he's spoken at NLP conferences; he's an academic psychologist who specialises in studying what works in influencing human beings, and especially the little psychological triggers that temporarily turn off our critical faculties and get us to accept things automatically. That's what's going on when you get to the 'science bit' in an advert for cosmetics or shampoo - scientists have come up with this, or it's endorsed by the British Skin Council (whoever they are), so it must work.

Another of Cialdini's principles of influence is called "Social Proof". This is the idea that you are more likely to buy something, or do something, when you see other people doing it. It's why you see testimonials for products or services on people's web sites. When you use extended quotes in a business context (rather than as Erickson used them, where his aim was to put people into a trance), they don't need to be that extended - something as simple as "One of our customers told me that their costs had reduced 30% in the three weeks since they installed the system" backs up your offer with a message from someone else. It's not you saying that, it's this other customer.

Switching Referential Index

Because these patterns were originally identified in academic linguistics, the names of the patterns lead people to think that they are more complicated than they actually are, but when you understand a pattern like this next one, you find that it's really quite simple.

All the pattern does is start off the sentence with one subject ('subject' in the sense of 'person or thing performing the action'), and then you switch the subject half way through, usually to make it more relevant or more distanced from the listener, whichever they need. I'll highlight the switching subjects in the next couple of examples so we can easily see how this works:

"*I* was quite nervous when I first started presenting, but I found that *you* relax as soon as you get into it."

"If *you're* expecting a bit of a tussle over this one, just take a moment to review the issues and I'm sure *we* can go into it in a positive frame of mind."

If readers aren't quite sure about this pattern yet, you can go back and identify where I sneaked in a couple of examples without explicitly identifying them when we first started talking about 'Switching Referential Index'. Will readers spot them? I'm sure you will.

One more thing about switching referential index. Some people habitually do this when they're talking about their own feelings. "Well, when that happened - you feel upset, don't you?" When I hear that, I wonder if they are attempting to dodge ownership of their own emotions by projecting them onto someone else. Maybe that's what it is, maybe it's just a habit they've got into. If someone does that a lot, you feel railroaded, and you get to the point where you think "I wish this person would take responsibility for their own feelings and stop trying legitimise it by trying to make out that I'm feeling the same way." Well, you might not, but I sometimes do.

Negative Suggestions

Now, I'm not sure I mentioned earlier on that the unconscious mind doesn't process negation. By negation I mean the idea of 'not' something.

You know that British tradition where people take their young children to the supermarket to punish them? You know what I'm talking about - "Don't touch those sweets!" And the young child, which below the age of about six is really an unconscious mind on legs, just hears "touch those sweets" because you can't form a mental image of 'not' something. And his unconscious mind goes "mmm... touch... those... sweets..." because that's the internal representation that the parent has just installed. And then he gets a stern telling off: "What did I just tell you? Don't touch those sweets!" And the kid starts to cry, because now he's in a double bind - he gets told off if he touches the sweets, but at the same time he really wants to because what his unconscious mind is taking from what the parent says is that image: "touch those sweets!"

The unconscious mind doesn't process negation - that's a logical, conscious-mind concept that you can't form a sensory internal representation of. "Don't think of a blue rhinoceros." Now I'm not suggesting that you wanted to think of a blue rhinoceros, but actually, you had to form some sort of representation of one in order to process what was said.

This realisation has couple of implications: first, if you want someone to do something, *tell them what you want them to do* rather than *what you don't want them to do*, because telling them what you don't want them to do just puts that internal representation in their minds. When I was doing my NLP trainer training assessments, one of my friends said "Whatever you do, don't get nervous, forget everything you know and make a complete fool of yourself." Very helpful! What he meant was, "Maintain your state, remember you've got all the knowledge you need, and do yourself justice."

Secondly, if you want a sneaky way of asking or getting someone to do something without appearing to do it explicitly - and I'm not suggesting you would ever do this in real life - you can use what's called a

"**Negative Suggestion**". "Don't buy until you're absolutely ready", "I wouldn't want you to take this unless it's the right thing for you", "I'm not saying that these shares are always going to go up in value".

I'm not suggesting that you start thinking about situations where you can use negative suggestions - but of course I am.

Negative Tag Questions

Now, I bet you're already familiar with this next pattern, aren't you? "Negative Tag Questions" are closed questions tagged onto the end of a sentence. On the surface these tag questions are seeking agreement with what's being said, but they also have the effect of displacing opposition, don't they? And that's how Erickson used them.

Our minds are programmed to pay more attention to questions than statements, aren't they? Because questions demand a response, do they not? So when a tag question is added to the end of a sentence, it diverts your attention there and makes it easier for what the sentence is saying to slide past any conscious examination or resistance, doesn't it?

Now you're alerted to this pattern, you'll be a lot more aware of it, won't you? These last few sentences, where I've used tag questions a lot to give you some examples, should also alert you to be careful about using them too much. The general rule with the Milton Model - or any NLP language pattern - is 'if it doesn't sound natural, you're overdoing it'. If the listener's conscious mind notices something unusual, it's put on the alert to critically examine what you are saying, which defeats the object of making suggestions at the unconscious level.

Milton Erickson, and hypnotherapists in general, can get away with a lot more in terms of weird language patterns than we can in everyday conversation, and much more than in business contexts like sales, where we are on our guard to some extent anyway. When a client goes to see a hypnotherapist, there's an implicit contract that whatever the therapist says is designed to help them, and also, people expect hypnotherapists to say strange things - not the case in everyday life.

With the tag question pattern, also be careful about using it if you are asking a question where you actually want a truthful answer - if you ask an interviewee "You've done this before, haven't you?" they might be tempted to say they have, just to go along with your suggestion.

Selectional Restriction Violation

Now, here's a pattern that delights in foxing most students of NLP, because usually, in my experience, the explanations are a bit stingy with good examples of how you can actually use it. But this book wants to be the best guide to language patterns anywhere, and it knows its job isn't done until you understand every pattern and how to make it work for you.

This pattern doesn't help itself by concealing its usefulness behind a name that mystifies rather than clarifies how the pattern works and when you can use it. "Selectional restriction violation" - it's keeping its cards pretty close to its chest, isn't it?

All it means is this: attributing qualities or actions to something that cannot, by its nature, possess them - especially attributing intentions or feelings to inanimate objects. For some reason most books on NLP don't give brilliant examples of this pattern - I can't really see myself saying "your notebook has learned many things" to my students - but actually people use this pattern all the time.

Have you ever had a morning where your car didn't want to start? Well actually, the car doesn't have any feelings about it one way or another - it's a lump of metal. And over time, computer systems get more user-friendly. Actually, the systems don't have any feelings about the users one way or another - but we all know what that expression means.

Two things about this pattern: the unconscious mind will apply these qualities or actions to itself, finding nowhere else to logically put them. So one of my students came up with a great example in a business context: "This system enjoys a lot of advantages over the competition." Yes, you could just say it has advantages, but why not get the word "enjoy" in there and psychologically prime the customer to feel a little bit better.

Secondly, this pattern appeals to "animism" - the primitive idea that every object has a mind – which is the way a child thinks. So using this pattern has something of an age-regression effect, which can be useful if you want people to see the world more vividly, be more creative or not overthink things.

You may want to jump back to the beginning of this section to find the examples of this pattern that I've concealed in there - they actually do want you to find them.

Now Practice!

So that's the Milton Model. If you were studying this with the aim of becoming a skilled hypnotherapist, what you would want to do now is to practice putting these patterns together in different ways, and practising making them up as you go along - in fact, letting your unconscious mind generate them for you - so that you can improvise suggestions in a connected and coherent way for any client, with any problem, without a script.

If you want to use the Milton Model in a business context, to increase sales or lead your team better, or you're a teacher, a manager or a coach who wants the most effective ways to communicate belief in people's capabilities, or a sports psychologist who wants to get the athlete into the best possible frame of mind to compete, here's what I suggest you do: get a notebook small enough to carry around with you, allocate a separate page to each pattern, and write down any real-life Milton Model examples that you hear that are relevant to what you want to do with them. In fact, just write down any good examples at all that you hear, or think up, because it's the structure of the pattern that's important, not the content. You can always substitute different words into the pattern to make it relevant to your purposes. If you attend a live NLP Practitioner training (the best and some would say the only way to really learn NLP, as opposed to learning *about* it) bring your examples into the course with you - doing this kind of practice is the most important quality that distinguishes the star performer from the average.

One final word about the Milton Model. When you are using it, you need to *pay attention*. Erickson had exquisite sensory acuity, not in the sense that he had eyes like a hawk or ears like a bat, but just that he noticed what was going on with the people that he worked with, so he noticed state changes, speeding up or slowing down of breathing or even heartbeats, skin colour changes and so on. These subtle changes told him when his clients were going into or coming out of trance, when a suggestion was particularly effective, and so on. That gave him a feedback loop that told him to do more of a particular kind of pattern, when to change tack, when to do a pattern interrupt, and so on. Other people thought he had almost magical powers. He was just paying attention.

In the same way, when you use Milton Model patterns, make sure you're not firing blind. Pay attention to the effect your words have, and remember that you're in a conversation. Your Milton Model patterns should make sense in the context of the conversation, and flow naturally from the other person's responses. That way, what you say will seem natural to the other person, won't jar the conversation off track, and the patterns can get on with doing their jobs.

How can you possibly get good enough to do that? Practice enough, and your unconscious mind will start coming up with the right patterns exactly when you need them, just as it generates the right words without you having to think about it when you're having a normal conversation.

7 METAPHORS

One more thing that you will sometimes see included in the Milton Model, but really deserves a whole section to itself, is metaphor. If you had to get the real essence of what metaphor is about, it's understanding and experiencing one kind of thing in terms of another.

This mechanism is tremendously important to our experience. Some psychologists believe that metaphor is fundamental to the way we think and express ourselves. We use metaphors all the time when we speak, mostly without noticing them: if someone says "*our relationship has hit a rocky patch*", they are using a metaphor where the relationship is like a vehicle that they are both travelling in, and the difficulties are like a rough bit of road. When we talk about someone *blowing their top*, that's a metaphor that says anger is like some kind of hot liquid, maybe molten lava, so the person is like a volcano. If you are *looking forward to something*, you are using a spatial metaphor for time, maybe as a road that you're travelling along. Or maybe you experience time as more like standing by a road, and events are vehicles on the road moving towards you - as in 'the summer holidays are nearly upon us'.

One important element when you're building rapport with someone is to listen to the metaphors people use. These can tell you a lot about how they are thinking, and matching those metaphors will help you to be understood and to feel like you're on the same wavelength.

That's one way of using metaphors. Milton Erickson had another way of using them. He would use stories to help his clients find resources within themselves, to bring about state changes, to help install new coping strategies, or to make a particular learning point for his students.

They could be real life stories from his life experience, from some hobby or interest of the client, stories of how other clients had solved problems, or drawn from myths or folk tales, or references to stories that the client was already familiar with from the Bible or even TV or Hollywood.

For example, Erickson was asked if he could do anything for Joe, a florist who was suffering from a particularly malignant form of cancer and had been given a month to live. Joe was, not surprisingly, unhappy and depressed at this news, and in addition was experiencing severe pain and found it hard to rest. A relative begged Erickson to give him hypnosis for pain relief; Erickson agreed, somewhat reluctantly as he doubted he could do much for the man, especially as Joe was known to be skeptical of and even hostile to the idea of hypnosis. However, he reasoned that if he conveyed by his presence that he was genuinely interested in Joe, and genuinely wanted to help him, that should at least provide some comfort.

As Joe loved growing things, Erickson decided to talk about a tomato plant: about how it grows, how the rains bring it *peace and comfort*, and how it can *feel comfortable* growing. He talked about how it took *just one day at a time*, how it could *know the feeling of comfort* each day, and how the tomato plant knew what it was doing, and how thinking of the luscious tomatoes beginning to form *could give you the desire to eat*.

In the course of the long story about how the tomato plant grows, Erickson interspersed many times in many different ways suggestions of comfort, ease, peace, all feeling well, taking it one day at a time, resting, and even increasing appetite - all sounding natural in the context of the story.

The hypnosis-skeptical Joe went into a trance listening to the story, and afterwards was most appreciative. During his remaining time he was more content, his physical condition improved (although the malignancy continued to progress), and the pain was much reduced, so he could come off his pain relief medication.

So what was Erickson doing as he told the tomato plant story? He noticed the patterns in the client's situation (that he was a florist who loved growing things, and was in pain and distress), and chunked laterally to something else that had some parallels (a tomato plant growing) and contained some additional resources (a sense of comfort and ease, taking each day as it comes). This allowed Joe's unconscious mind to reframe his experience as something less distressing.

Metaphors are understanding and experiencing a thing, or a feeling, or a situation, in terms of something else that is analogous. The internal logic of the metaphor sets limits on what we expect to happen, and on the choices the person sees in that situation. So if someone feels they have *painted themselves into a corner*, just stopping and walking out of there won't seem like a valid option to them. Even if in real life that choice is available, they won't feel able to do it, because they are experiencing the situation in terms of the metaphor as much as they are terms of their sensory experience.

One reason that metaphors are so powerful is that we can use them to talk about things that are hard to express in any other way - things in our lives that are mysterious, intangible, loaded with meaning - in a short, vivid, compact analogy drawn from our concrete experience. As long as the relationships in the metaphor are analogous, we don't have to describe the real situation in detail - we can work out the rest of the information from the metaphor. So metaphors can carry a huge amount of information about what an experience is like in a few words.

So, you can use metaphors for understanding other people better and strengthening rapport with them, you can use them as Erickson did as a way of activating a person's unconscious resources and giving them new choices, and you can also use them for describing a complex issue in a few words or an image that sticks in people's minds, getting people to see something in a different way, or in a presentation leading your audience through a series of emotions from where they start out to where you want them to end up. Would that be a useful item to have in your leadership toolbox?

How To Create Metaphors

Here's how you can create metaphors quickly and easily. The basic steps to generate a metaphor for helping someone to resolve a problem or have more choices are as follows:

1. Identify the **present situation** or issue, and the **desired state** or outcome. This could be moving from a complex issue that is hard to understand

to a simple image that everyone can make sense of and remember; from a problem to a solution; from an unhelpful emotion in an audience (such as suspicion) to a helpful emotion (such as curiosity); or from a perceived situation of no choices to one where choices are available.

2. Notice the significant people/places/things in the situation, and the relationships between them.

3. Keeping the desired state in mind, chunk up from the present state to a category by asking yourself: "What is this situation/issue an example of?"

4. Chunk down from there by asking yourself: "What is another example of this category of situation or issue that includes the possibility of ending up in the desired state?"

5. Find analogies for the significant people/places/things and for the relationships between them. In the jargon, the metaphor should be 'isomorphic' (from the Greek, meaning 'the same shape as') with the real situation; in other words, the structure of the relationships between the elements, and the logic of the whole, should be the same, even though the content may be quite different.

For example, John Grinder uses the example of coaching a business owner who is engaged in a dispute with a former business partner over the ownership of a business. All of the business guy's energy is going into the dispute, and he's neglecting all sorts of other opportunities that would actually make him more money. So in Grinder's example, you might use a story about two hummingbirds fighting over a flower, while taking no notice of all the other flowers all around them.

Notice that you don't have to resolve the story for them - you don't talk about the two hummingbirds making up, or one of them flying away and getting loads more nectar from the other flowers. The possibilities are there, and you leave it to the person's unconscious mind to find the best possibilities for them - which may include some choice, action or idea that you hadn't thought of.

Also, keep the elements in the story relevant; one of the business people might be married, but unless the spouse was also a significant player in the situation, you wouldn't start talking about one of the hummingbirds sharing a nest.

Ideally, the metaphor will appeal to the values or interests of the listener, to keep them engaged. So the hummingbird metaphor will work best with someone who is interested in ornithology, or who is looking forward to a tropical holiday.

6. Finally, tell the story (or mention the metaphor if it's a short one) and notice the response you get.

If you are familiar with the NLP technique of 'anchoring', you can anchor problem states and resources within the story using voice tone, facial expression or even touch. Memorable images within the story can become anchors for resources. You can also embed positive suggestions, as Erickson did in his tomato plant story.

Where you are just coming up with a metaphor to help someone understand a complex situation, rather than for coaching or therapy purposes, you can simplify this process a bit - just ask yourself "What is this situation like?" This question leads you to chunk sideways - your unconscious mind will handle the 'chunking up' and 'chunking down to another example' steps, and you will know if you have a good example if it feels right. Check the response that your metaphor gets though, and be prepared to change it - what feels right to you may not work within the listener's map of the world.

Metaphors don't have to be longwinded - as little as one word in the right place may evoke a symbol with a wealth of meaning attached. Because of the impact of psychological priming, you're usually going to want to keep the internal representations positive to elicit positive states in the listener. This is also worth bearing in mind when you use Milton Model suggestions generally.

Finally, before you use your metaphor on an audience, especially in a set-piece presentation or speech, put yourself in the shoes of the audience and listen to it from their point of view. Is it something they can relate to? Is there any other way that it could be taken? This will help you to avoid unintended reactions and unexpected laughs.

8 HOW TO LEARN MORE

Attend A Live Training

The absolute best way to learn to do NLP, as opposed to learning *about* it, is to attend a good NLP Practitioner course. I should qualify that and say a good live NLP practitioner course, ideally 'in the room' rather than online, as there are unfortunately many self-paced video courses describing themselves as 'NLP Practitioner Certification training' nowadays.

You *cannot* learn to do NLP from self-paced video courses. There is no substitute for properly designed live exercises, with the opportunity for feedback from your fellow participants and from a trainer who knows what he or she is doing. Therefore, I would go for a small-group course (numbers up to around 16), and with enough time to practice and ask questions. I would say a decent course needs a minimum of 8 days.

Although I'm mostly writing books and doing corporate training and coaching these days, **I will run more courses in the UK if there is a demand** - email me at andy@coachingleaders.co.uk to let me know you are interested, and once there are enough people interested in an area, we can arrange the timing of the course to suit you. Also, I like to travel, so if you can find a minimum of six people in your area who are prepared to commit to taking the course, I can come to your country to train your group.

Other trainers around the world I recommend: Jonathan Altfeld, Doug O'Brien, and Debra Heslin on the East coast of the USA; Robert Dilts and Judith DeLozier on the West coast; Jeremy Lazarus, Elizabeth Pritchard, and Melody Cheal in the UK; James Tsakalos in Australia; and Richard Bolstad in New Zealand (also trains in various locations worldwide).

Practice

Even if you haven't attended a live training yet, you can sharpen your NLP language skills by constant practice. Notice examples of Meta Model patterns in your own internal dialogue and in what other people say, in conversation, on the radio, on the TV; and in what they write, in books, in newspapers and magazines, and on the internet. Politicians are a particularly fertile source of deletions, distortions and generalisations!

Keep a notebook of the most Milton Model patterns and the most striking metaphors that you encounter. And look for an NLP practice group or meetup group near you. And once you've taken an NLP Practitioner training, keep practicing - it's what distinguishes the very best NLP practitioners from the rest.

Further reading, viewing and listening

If you haven't read it already, you're going to want to read the first book in this series, *Practical NLP: How to Use NLP Principles to Improve Your Life and Work, Even if You're Not NLP Trained*. Get it from the Practical NLP website at nlppod.com.

The Structure of Magic Volume 1 by Richard Bandler and John Grinder is a must-read if you're interested in in-depth study of the Meta Model. It's written mainly for therapists, but the patterns apply equally for business use.

Patterns of the Hypnotic Techniques of Milton H. Erickson, M.D. Volume 1 and *Volume 2* by Richard Bandler and John Grinder are for the most obsessive NLP language geeks only, I would say - for a much more accessible guide to Ericksonian patterns for hypnotherapists I would recommend *Wordweaving: The Science of Suggestion - A Comprehensive Guide to Creating Hypnotic Language* by my friend Trevor Silvester. And for using Ericksonian (and other) NLP language patterns for persuasion, it's worth reading the *Persuasion Skills Black Book: Practical NLP Language Patterns for Getting The Response You Want* by my equally talented friend Rintu Basu.

For learning more about the role metaphors play in our thinking, take a look at *Metaphors We Live By* or the very weighty *Philosophy In The Flesh*, both by George Lakoff and Mark Johnson.

You can find links to order all of these on my 'Books about NLP language patterns' page at: nlppod.com/books-about-nlp-language-patterns/

If you prefer to listen while you learn, subscribe to the Practical NLP Podcast at nlppod.com.

Visit coachingleaders.co.uk for more tips, book reviews, research news and information about emotional intelligence, coaching, leadership, and related subjects. You can also subscribe to the free Coaching Leaders Newsletter there.

Finally, if you have any questions or feedback about this book, please do contact me at andy@coachingleaders.co.uk

Andy Smith

Treignac, March 2022

INDEX

A

Abstraction, 31, 32, 37, 38, 39, 40, 41, 42, 43, 56, 93
Ambiguity, 103
Analogue Marker, 108, 110
Animism, 120

B

Bandler, Richard, 3, 14, 46, 47, 51, 52, 74, 79, 82, 97, 111, 112, 135
Basu, Rintu, 136

C

Cause and Effect, 52, 58, 85
Change
    Generative, 3
    Remedial, 3
Chomsky, Noam, 8
Cialdini, Robert, 113
Comparative Deletions, 71, 72, 96
Complex Equivalence, 54, 58, 88
Conversational Postulates, 109

D

Deep Structure and Surface Structure, 7
Deletion, 8
Distortions, 8

E

Embedded Suggestions, 107
Erickson, Milton, 24, 39, 40, 79, 82, 97, 101, 102, 106, 108, 112, 113, 117, 118, 121, 124, 125, 126, 127, 130, 135
Extended Quote, 111

G

Generalisations, 8, 58
Grinder, John, 3, 14, 46, 47, 51, 67, 74, 79, 82, 97, 128, 135

I

Influence, 11, 12, 51, 79, 80, 81, 83, 84, 87, 88, 107, 113
Internal representation, 7
Intonation, 110, 111

J

James, Tad, 14, 42, 111, 134

L

Langer, Ellen, 85
Lost Performatives, 50, 58, 84

M

Meta Model, 45
  Deletions, 66
  Distortions, 48
  Generalisations, 58
Metaphor, 123, 124, 126, 127, 135, 136
Metaprogram, 33
Milton Model, 79, 81, 82, 83, 84, 85, 88, 90, 95, 96, 97, 98, 99, 118, 120, 121, 122, 123, 130, 135
  Deletions, 92
  Distortions, 84
  Generalisations, 90
  Indirect Suggestions, 103
  Pacing, 97
Mind Reading, 49, 58, 84
Modal Operators, 63, 66, 91
Modelling, 46

N

Negative Suggestions, 115
Negative Tag Questions, 117
Nominalisations, 66, 67, 69, 71, 92

P

Pacing, 85, 98
Paralanguage, 76
Perls, Fritz, 46, 47
Presuppositions, 11, 14, 15, 19, 21, 27, 57, 58, 89, 90
  Adverb/Adjective, 23
  Awareness, 20
  Cause and Effect, 18
  Complex Equivalence, 19
  Existence, 14
  Inclusive/Exclusive Or, 24
  Necessity, 16
  Ordinal, 26
  Possibility, 16
  Time, 21
Presuppositions of NLP, 5
Principles of NLP, 4
Pucelik, Frank, 3

S

Satir, Virginia, 46, 47
Selectional Restriction Violation, 118

INDEX

Sensory Acuity, 121
Silvester, Trevor, 135
Simple Deletions, 70, 72, 94
Switching Referential Index, 114

T

Transformational Grammar, 8
Truisms, 102

U

Unconscious Mind, 4, 8, 40, 79, 80, 82, 83, 87, 97, 101, 103, 107, 108, 109, 110, 111, 112, 115, 116, 118, 119, 120, 122, 126, 127, 129, 130
Universal Quantifiers, 65, 90
Unspecified Nouns, 70, 72, 95
Unspecified Referential Index. *See* Unspecified Noun
Unspecified Verbs, 69, 72, 93
Utilisation, 101, 102

V

Value Judgments, 50, 58, 90

ABOUT THE AUTHOR

Andy Smith is an NLP trainer, Appreciative Inquiry facilitator, and Emotional Intelligence coach who has trained and coached director-level clients in the UK, the Middle East, and South East Asia. He specialises in helping leaders and teams get beyond the blocks that stop them achieving their potential. Andy is the author of *Achieve Your Goals: Strategies To Transform Your Life* (Dorling Kindersley 2006) and the *Practical NLP, Practical Coaching Guides* and *Quick Personal Development* e-book series. To see all of Andy's books and e-books, visit the Practical NLP website at nlppod.com.

Andy is a serial NLP practice group founder. He started the Richmond NLP Group (along with Nick Driscoll) in 1996 and it's still going strong, having been through a couple of changes of management. He also started the Manchester NLP Group and the Manchester Business NLP and Emotional Intelligence Group, all of which have given countless people their first step on their NLP journey.

In addition to the Practical NLP e-book series, Andy has developed an acclaimed activity pack for NLP trainers, *The NLP Trainer's Exercise Pack*, as well as customisable and rebrandable NLP course manuals that will save newly-qualified trainers weeks of effort. You can find these resources at: webstore.coachingleaders.co.uk.

Website, blog and podcast: nlppod.com

Online store: webstore.coachingleaders.co.uk

Twitter: @PracticalNLP

Contact: andy@coachingleaders.co.uk

www.ingramcontent.com/pod-product-compliance
Lightning Source LLC
Chambersburg PA
CBHW031920240526
45464CB00021B/605